Assessing Learners in Higher Education

Sally Brown and Peter Knight

KOGAN PAGE

London • Philadelphia

Teaching and Learning in Higher Education Series
Series Editor: John Stephenson

500 Tips for Tutors Phil Race and Sally Brown
Assessment in Higher Education Sally Brown and Peter Knight
Case Studies on Teaching in Higher Education Peter Schwartz and Graham Webb
Practical Pointers for University Teachers Bill Cox
Using Learning Contracts in Higher Education John Stephenson and
　　Mike Laycock
Using Records of Achievement in Higher Education Alison Assiter and Eileen Shaw
Assessing Learners in Higher Education Sally Brown and Peter Knight

First published in 1994

Reprinted 1997

Kogan Page Limited
120 Pentonville Road
London N1 9JN

British Library Cataloguing in Publication Data

A CIP record for this book is available from the British Library.
ISBN 0 7494 1113 9

Typeset by Saxon Graphics Ltd, Derby

Printed and bound in Great Britain by Biddles Ltd, Guildford and King's Lynn.

Contents

Acknowledgements

Our thanks to Michael Armstrong, Garth Rhodes, Peter Dove, Mark Dobbins, Lesley Dalby and Jackie Costello at the University of Northumbria at Newcastle; and, at Lancaster, to Cath Baldwin and Karl Turner who have allowed us to draw on their work, and to John Wakeford for unfailing support and encouragement. Chris Rust of Oxford Brookes University and Phil Race of the University of Glamorgan have both helped shape our thinking.

Peter Knight and Sally Brown,
Lancaster and Newcastle.

Preface

Few issues are currently exciting more attention in teaching and learning in higher education than is assessment. Just at the time when academics are having to cope with increasing student numbers against a fixed or falling unit of resource, the focus upon competence-based learning is causing us to radically re-examine our assessment practices. Simultaneously, there is a shift, partly driven by the enterprise initiative, towards assessment of students' transferable personal skills as well as the academic content of what they are studying. All of this is leading to the development of new assessment methods, giving rise to the need for greater than ever ingenuity and flexibility, while still monitoring and assuring the quality of the process.

In this book we explore the key issues of assessment: who is it for? What modes of assessment exist? What makes for sound assessment and why do we assess anyway? What are the agencies that are promoting innovative methods of assessment in the first place and what are the catalysts for change?

We assert that formative assessment is a central element of learning, in that the feedback students receive enables them to develop and extend themselves in ways that end-point assessment cannot.

At the core of our text we provide descriptions of a wide variety of techniques for assessment, together with some guidance on how and when best to use them, while at the same time recognizing some of the pitfalls that can arise. We provide practical suggestions on how to assess better, including specific advice on the use of explicit criteria – the key, we believe, to improved student performance. All assessment methods, traditional or otherwise, disadvantage some students so we recommend the adoption of diverse methods to remedy inequalities as far as possible.

Increasingly, students are becoming involved in their own and each other's assessment and we argue strongly for this practice as a means not only of providing feedback to students but also of developing within students the capability better to judge their own abilities and performance, providing them with the opportunities to develop skills for learning that will be of value long after they leave the university.

Most universities are coping with these demands in a piecemeal manner, with innovation and good practice rarely being implemented or disseminated in a systematic fashion. We argue for the need for assessment systems for universities, in order to inculcate a strategic approach to assessment, without stifling individuality and local decision making.

We feel that this is a timely and, we hope, useful book in that it brings together many of the central ideas current in the field of assessment at the moment. We have built our work on research and knowledge of good practice in our own and other universities, and we are always interested in hearing from others working in the field who have ideas to share with us.

Part 1: Issues of assessment

Curriculum design, assessment and evaluation begin at the same point (Heywood, 1989, p.23).

Murdering the Innocents
Thomas Gradgrind, sir . . . A man who proceeds on the principle that two and two are four, and nothing over, and who is not to be talked into allowing for anything over . . . Thomas Gradgrind . . . With a rule and a pair of scales, and the multiplication table always in his pocket, sir, ready to weigh and parcel any measure of human nature, and tell you exactly what it comes to. It is a mere question of figures (Charles Dickens, Hard Times).

Chapter 1:

Distinctions and Definitions

Assessment and fattening pigs

Pigs are not fattened by being weighed, as critics of assessment are quick to point out. Why invest time, thought and money in assessing students thoroughly, when it would be better to concentrate on the business of teaching, or upon research? Surely pressure for assessment reform is just another example of *them* trying to hog-tie *us*, finding busy-work for us to do, work which will produce information which will probably not be used or, if it is used, will somehow be used against us, rather like the league tables have been used against schools?

In days when professionalism seems to be threatened, whether the profession is medicine, law, social work, nursing or policing, this view is understandable. Assessment data may well be used, as they have been in schools, to ensure compliance with some policy or another. When resources are tight and when growing group sizes threaten to reduce tutors to coping, then it is self-evidently sensible to concentrate on the core business, which we will take to be teaching – although we well recognize that for some academics teaching is an embarrassing distraction from research, but that is another issue. How, then, can we claim that assessment not only matters but that assessment reform is the most urgent priority confronting under-graduate education?

You don't cure a patient by taking his or her temperature, nor climb a mountain by reading a map, nor do you become a better higher education (HE) mathematics tutor by reading about theories of motivation. Yet each activity supplies information which is useful if not necessary for the successful completion of the task. I may try to make a diagnosis and to prescribe without knowing a patient's temperature, but it is hardly scientific or sensible to do so. Climbing a mountain without knowing the terrain is plain foolish, albeit possible in favourable circumstances. Teaching mathematics without a grasp of the range of classroom management techniques is also possible, but circumscribed and inefficient.

The weakest claim is that much the same could be said of undergraduate studies which had only a small assessment component. It is quite possible that students would learn, but without information about what they knew, understood and could do, intuition would guide the lecturers' activities and we might expect inefficiencies to prevail. Moreover, if tutors had not thought about assessment, there is every chance of a narrow, rather well-worn range of assessment techniques being used to assess something – probably no one would be too sure what was being assessed. Indeed, it might be far from clear why any assessment was taking place, tradition and a moral sense that students *should* be assessed alone accounting for the continuing rounds of work written to be marked and forgotten. The weak claim is that assessment provides information about student learning which allows for a better match between what students *are required to do* and what they *can do*. Assessment, then, is a source of efficiency in teaching.

We, however, want to make a much stronger claim. Assessment is at the heart of the undergraduate experience. Assessment defines what students regard as important, how they spend their time, and how they come to see themselves as students and then as graduates. It follows, then, that it is not the curriculum which shapes assessment, but assessment which shapes the curriculum and embodies the purposes of higher education. By assessment we mean a

systematic basis for making inferences about the learning and development of students . . . the process of defining, selecting, designing, collecting, analyzing, interpreting and using information to increase students' learning and development
(Erwin, 1991, p.15).

As we shall show, there are considerable pressures on HE to demonstrate exactly what the state gets for its enormous investment, and those pressures are for universities to show that they are not simply producing social science graduates, say, but that these graduates have developed abilities which are of general value, that is that they have developed what might be called general competences, enterprise skills or the qualities fostered by a liberal education. In order to demonstrate that, universities need to be assessing the degree to which graduates can display those abilities, and in order to promote those abilities, universities need to have in place assessment arrangements which ensure that the curriculum as taught and received actually does make students work at them. Assessment, then, is central to meeting the pressure upon HE institutions.

This book develops these two main ideas: that assessment provides information for better learning and teaching; and that assessment reform is necessary if universities are to ensure and to show that graduates have achievements of the sort wanted by government, employers, funding bodies, tax-payers, and by the students themselves. In these times of public accountability and consumer power, we shall explain that assessment is central to universities' practices for total quality management, practices which are going to become increasingly important in financially straitened and highly competitive times. We also provide a range of assessment methods to encourage universities to assess in ways that are fit for the intended purposes.

Who is assessment for?

A recurring message is that assessment may be many things for many people, for example:

- the student
- other students
- tutors
- mentors
- employers
- university management
- financing and other government bodies
- funding councils.

Depending on those people's interests, assessment needs to:

- take different forms
- have different levels of reliability and validity
- be done at different points in students' undergraduate careers
- have its findings communicated in different ways.

Implicit in this is the idea that assessments have different purposes which, we shall show, has potent implications.

Different audiences want different data for different purposes at different times. A student may well want feedback to enable him or her to work on points in need of attention rather than to keep practising points of strength. Employers may want accounts of what the student can do and the student him or herself, towards the end of his or her studies, will also want such a summative verdict. University management will want information about how much students have gained from their undergraduate years, but mentors, to take another audience, will initially need to know what the student may be trusted to do and where the main points for care and development lie.

Not only are there different purposes for assessment, but these purposes are neither separate nor entirely compatible. There is a tension between assessment which is done in the spirit of working with someone, much as we work together on writing this book, so that the aim is to review, refine and learn, and assessment as a score which has been judged to be a fair summary of one's achievement, and which may simply be presented as one number, the symbol of three years' work. Furthermore, at any one time it is likely that assessment will be trying to serve more than one master for more than one purpose. It is hardly surprising that assessment is a complex matter, as is curriculum: both should reflect the simultaneous demands of multiple audiences for multiple purposes. It follows that assessment systems will need to be extensive, sophisticated and complex if they are to begin to meet the legitimate demands of all of these audiences.

Notice the implication that all students are affected by the demands of these audiences. Looking at assessment cannot, then, be left to the enterprise of individuals or departments responding to particular enthusiasms. In Part 4 we show that an institutional approach, which ought to support and channel rather than to dragoon academic initiative, is necessary.

We confidently say that assessment systems as we have sketched them here are not normally found in the UK and we argue that substantial reform is necessary if HE is to be seen to meet legitimate demands upon it.

Perspectives on the business of assessment

We might start with a simple model of assessment which identifies two interest groups as prime markers on a spectrum. This is not to preclude other ways of analysing the modes and purposes of assessment, but it is a convenient way of introducing some key ideas.

One group comprises the technicians, very much concerned with the techniques of measurement. Their influence has varied over time, their techniques do vary. However, their interest is in devising a more reliable way of measuring – a better tool.

Reliability

'Reliability' refers to the attempt to make sure that any assessment result describes the phenomenon being assessed and is not a product of the measurement instrument used. So, trying to measure a piece of fabric with an elastic tape-measure is an unreliable procedure: using a yardstick is reliable. Reliability is about consistency of measurement and comes in several forms. One is the reliability of the assessor – does this person agree with others who are equally expert? If there is a lot of disagreement, then there is also low inter-observer reliability.

A second form relates to different measuring devices – do they agree? After all, we expect all 25cm rules to give the same readings and if they don't the instruments themselves have low reliability, *always given that they all claim to be measuring the same thing*.

A third form is test-retest reliability. A single measure should give the same answer if it measures the same, unchanged object on different occasions. An elastic tape-measure lacks test-retest reliability.

Reliability is a concept much associated with psychology, and in psychology there are those who have argued that it is often bought at the cost of devising measures which are trivial and artificial, rather like measuring the length of a piece of cloth when the buyer is interested in the fabric and colour. Moreover, test-retest reliability may be heightened at a cost to sensitivity in detecting changes that *have* happened. In human affairs it is far from obvious that test-retest reliability is important, since people change and are changing. And if two tests give similar scores, do we need two? Where is the advantage in devising two similar measures?

Moreover, reliability was not intended to be a concept applied to dichotomous data, as with criterion-referenced assessment where the candidate has either met or not met the requirements set out in the criterion. A further statistical complication is that problems arise when sample sizes are small. An assessment might be given to just 25 students; statistical techniques can handle such low numbers, but they are not at their best under those circumstances.

It seems as if the notion of reliability in HE assessment is being displaced by the concept of quality assurance in assessment, which emphasizes the need for *procedures* designed to ensure that assessments are as fair as possible. Of course, renaming something doesn't make it easier to do, but with quality assurance there is more emphasis on having in place reliable procedures than reliable tests, which may simplify things somewhat.

However, on a national scale there is a strong case for wanting reliable, end-of-course measures of student achievement, for if it is not possible to believe that a 2:1 degree from the University of Utopia is equivalent to a 2:1 degree from Arcadia University, then a whole series of desirable assumptions collapses. Notice that this is a claim only about end-of-course measures.

A second group is the practitioners, people who have to apply and use assessment techniques for practical purposes as a part of their work. In this context we can take teachers as an example, but one might equally take medical practitioners or social workers. Their concerns are with practicality, accessibility and effectiveness, and they can be impatient with the technicians' perpetual cries that really nothing is certain enough. They need to be able to use assessments, even if the assessments may not be as reliable as the ideal prescribes. Here we need to introduce three further concepts, since practitioners are concerned with more than just reliability.

The purposes of assessment – summative and formative

The first two, *summative* and *formative* assessment, describes the purposes of assessment. Summative assessment includes end-of-course assessment and essentially means that this is assessment which produces a measure which sums up someone's achievement and which has no other real use except as a description of what has been achieved. Formative assessment is where the purpose is to get an estimate of achievement which is used to help in the learning process. Diagnostic assessment may be regarded as a sub-set of formative assessment. Formative assessment also includes course-work where the student receives feedback which helps him/her to improve their next performance; discussion between a mentor and a student; and end-of-module examinations whose results are used to identify areas for attention in later modules.

It will be appreciated that formative and summative assessment may share the same methods and, in theory, a measurement may have both formative and summative purposes. However, the differences in purpose do not sit well together because with summative assessment there is a premium on reliability, since these are results which have to be communicated in a final form to the world at large: meanings must be clear, standards known and reliability assured. Typically, these summative judgements are simply communicated, perhaps as a grade-point average, as an 'A' level grade, or as a percentage. With formative assessment there is a sense in which the assessment is always provisional, since it is to be discussed and negotiated as a part of the process of using the data to improve performance.

Some practitioners prefer to say that summative assessment counts towards degree classification, whereas formative doesn't. While we do not see this as the key distinction, it is worth noticing. If we plot the two sets of distinctions on a chart, we get the pattern shown in Figure 1.1, which has the merit of reminding us that the summative/formative distinction is not a simple 'all-or-nothing' distinction. There are many blends of purpose, reflecting the multiple assessment audiences and the large number of ways of assessing learning. 'Formative' and 'summative' are useful tags, but no more.

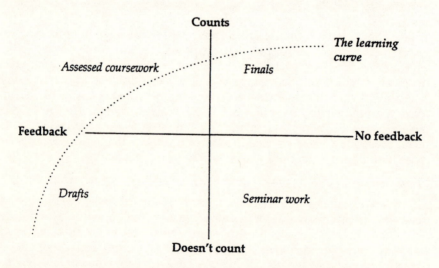

Figure 1.1 *Two dimensions of formative and summative assessment*

It is important to emphasize that formative and summative refer to the purposes of assessment rather than to the methods. Almost all of the methods reviewed in Chapter 2 are neutral, in that they can be applied to summative or formative ends. Often the mistake is made of assuming that it is the method which is summative or formative, and not the purpose. This, we suggest, is a serious mistake because it turns the assessor's attention away from the crucial issue of feedback. If the assessor believes that a method is formative, he or she may fall into the trap of using the method – a piece of coursework done half way through a module – without taking the time to go over with the student the implications of the assessment. If that piece of coursework is marked, returned and just stored away, then its effective use has been summative, whatever the intention had been. Nor are we convinced that the rather skimpy written comments which adorn many pieces of coursework count as feedback worthy of the name. The moral is quite simply that if formative assessment is to be taken seriously, then adequate feedback and review procedures need to be designed in, working in the spirit of total quality management.

Validity

Validity has the primary meaning of measuring what you set out to measure. Length is not a valid test of the quality of a fabric and degree examinations are not valid tests of a student's employment potential (well, most of them are not, since they measure only some of the things which will affect a student's effectiveness in daily working life). However, if we do have valid measures, there is the snag that they may not be reliable. For example, we may wish to know about students' attitudes, about their creativity, initiative, problem-solving ability, critical thinking and other such amorphous and very context-dependent powers. Or we might particularly want to look at the process by which students set about problems, issues and challenges.

Unfortunately, it is notoriously difficult to establish reliable measures of people's ways of working, of their attitudes, creativity, and such like. Reliability can be high when we try to measure some of the products of study, but validity may be a more appropriate concept to value when we talk of assessing the processes of study. A reliable test of problem solving might be artificial and detached from the rich disciplinary background which one would expect an engineering student, say, to draw upon. A valid test might be a good basis for discussion with students about their learning but have little meaning to others, such as employers, for example, since it is highly context-bound and provisional.

It also follows that valid measures relate to what students have done – to the delivered curriculum – rather than to some notion of what they should have done. Take 'A' levels, where, despite the existence of a syllabus, the examinations have little validity for many students, since topics which they grasp well do not appear on the paper and topics which they have (reasonably) missed do appear. For this reason degree examinations at all except the largest universities have greater validity, since tutors set questions which students should be able to answer. However, there is a cost in reliability, since nationally a great range of questions of varying levels of difficulty is set. Only the rather ramshackle external examiner system acts to bring some inter-institutional reliability to the system. (There are grounds for believing that the great improvement in students' degree classification is due in some measure to increases in the validity of assessments at the expense of reliability – Knight, 1991.)

Using assessment – another view of validity

A colleague at Lancaster University has developed the meaning of validity to embrace the idea that assessments should not only measure what they are designed to measure but that they should also have intended effects. All assessment affects our learning, and Ridgway's concern (1992) is that the likely effects should be considered when assessments are being devised. This is an important point for us, since we are arguing that the HE curriculum can be reformed by reforming the assessment system: what Heywood (1989) has called assessment-led innovation.

Ridgway proposed five further aspects of validity, which essentially remind us that assessment embodies certain educational, moral, philosophical and political values. The intention is to encourage changes in behaviour through assessment arrangements. He offers the 'corruption coefficient' as a measure of subversion, of the extent to which scores can be raised on a particular measure without changing the phenomena which the measures are supposed to relate to – for example, learners' scores can be manipulated easily by subtly adjusting task demands without teaching any differently.

The current tendency is to value validity more than reliability, but to demonstrate this it is necessary to introduce three further terms, *norm-referenced*, *criterion-referenced* and *ipsative assessments*.

Assessment benchmarks

Norm-referenced assessments describe where performances lie in relation to other performances. So, Utopia university may have one of the best macramé departments in the country, but none of them are much good, particularly compared to Japanese universities. Likewise, with a score of 8, Jean may be about average in her group, but since they're at Oxford, it means that she is one of the best students in the country at that subject. Equally, Najwa may have a 2:1 degree in law – so in norm-referenced terms she is quite good – but there are some areas where she is almost totally ignorant: the summative grade tells nothing about what she does well, what she does competently, and what she barely knows.

Norm referencing tells us little about anything, except the student's ability in relation to another group of students of unknown characteristics.

Criterion referencing means that people are assessed against pre-defined criteria. In a number of professions – nursing, teaching, social work – attempts are being made to express the competences which together comprise skill, and to describe these in terms of criteria. Thus the curriculum can be tuned to ensure that these criteria are deliberately fostered, and it will therefore become evident when a person has met a criterion, hence when competence is attained. Criterion referencing not only directs the curriculum, it also focuses assessment and allows for full descriptions of what a person has achieved. Moreover, this approach lends itself well to formative assessment, since it constitutes an agenda for discussion. Validity is at a premium, since assessment should be geared to showing whether a student can fulfil a criterion which the curriculum has been designed to enhance. There are, however, formidable problems with criteria-referenced assessment, as we shall see.

Ipsative assessment must be criterion-referenced. It simply means that the scale of worth, the benchmark against which current performance is measured, is oneself: present performance is compared to past performance. In running, the concept of a 'personal best' is an example of ipsative assessment. I may be a slow, gawky runner, unlikely ever to reach any of the criteria which are normally used to assess worth amongst runners. However, what matters to me (ipsative referencing) is the way in which my performance compares with past performance. My estimates may be subjective (I feel easier in my running than I did) or they may be very reliable (times over the same circuit); they may be formative (running style) or summative (total distance run per week); what is at issue is the way in which these data are understood, which with ipsative assessment is in relation to my other performances. Nor does this mean that continual improvement is sought. As I decay, simply maintaining some levels of activity is a goal worth having.

Reliability again

The current preference for validity over reliability is associated with the movement to criteria-referenced assessments, where it matters above all that assessment addresses all of the criteria – that it is valid, since otherwise the whole exercise is pointless. Reliability, then, would need to be re-defined (Johnson and Blinkhorn, 1992). In part the argument is that reliability is a concept which was developed in psychometrics where a number of assumptions about the purposes of assessment and the nature of the data were made. Those assumptions, it is claimed, do not hold good with criteria-referenced assessments, where the question is quite simply whether the best evidence is that the student has demonstrated the required competence. The exercise is a 'goodness of fit' exercise and reliability, then, is a question as to whether the matching of evidence against the criteria is well done. Now, most assessments will fall short of ideal standards (the 'best' assessment), and the question becomes 'whether the typical or everyday assessment processes are sufficiently accurate when compared with the best assessments that could be made' (*ibid.* p.12). The issue of cost. then, is implicated in the search for reliability, which becomes a matter of looking at the process of measuring 'goodness of fit' between performance and criteria and deciding on the boundaries of acceptability. Johnson and Blinkhorn (1992, p.13) suggest that the following should be considered:

- agreement amongst assessors
- the equivalence of different assessment processes
- the adequacy of different rules for establishing sufficiency of evidence
- the agreement of typical or everyday assessments with criterion assessments
- the extent to which claims are met.

Reliability may be reconceived as a process of assessing well against certain criteria. This is attractive to HE, since it puts a premium on validity and, because validity has to be judged in the context of each academic programme, it thereby consolidates the autonomy which HE institutions so value. If universities adopt this process approach to reliability, there is the danger that they will carefully make estimates of student performance against criteria which vary sharply from institution to institution, so that consumers will have little idea of what the reliable process means. And one important function of reliability is to guarantee a meaning, so that we can believe that, by and large, a 2:1 degree in Peace Studies at the University of Valhalla has required similar assessed performances to the same degree awarded by Asgard Polytechnic.

Attempts to discount reliability in its classical sense cannot be entirely successful, unless we are content with Erwin's observation on the American system (1991, p.54): 'of course, what is mastery at one institution is not the same at another institution'.

It is possible that reliability will come to mean fair and valid assessments against nationally-set criteria, such as NVQ Level 5 might provide. Even there, however, we would want to see a system for ensuring that assessors in different institutions were using similar sorts of evidence in similar ways in arriving at their judgements. A way of doing this would be to introduce a form of cross-institutional moderation, the successor, perhaps, to the external examiner system.

This can be illustrated by comparing degree assessments with 'A' levels. GCE boards expect full and detailed coursework records to be kept and require that this work is moderated to iron out the possible bias which any one examining centre might have towards its own candidates. Coursework marks are also compared to examination marks and adjusted in the case of excessive disparity. The examinations are marked by people who do not know the students, following tight mark schemes which have come from an early analysis of a sample of the exam answers. Markers attend standardization meetings, where they practise using the mark schemes. A sample of each marker's work is reviewed by the chief examiner and the whole batch is re-marked if need be. Grades are matched to mark ranges with the help of examination board statisticians, who have a view of the comparability of performance between different subjects and between different syllabi in the same subject. Boards commission studies to discover whether they award too few or too many 'A' levels and to see whether their grade distributions are defensible. On degree courses assessment is rarely so systematically approached.

Where reliability is not the main objective, there is no need to have double-marking, nor indeed to have grades. What is needed is information which may be fed back to students in ways which stimulate them to learn about what they might learn better. Adopting the total quality management approach might mean that only for summative assessments would the expensive processes of maximizing reliability have to be brought into play.

Coursework assessment shows some of the tensions which can arise between reliability and validity, between formative and summative assessment. Its formative function means that students should be encouraged to treat assessments as learning opportunities, to choose their own problems, take risks, try out ideas and insights and respond to the problem at whatever length and in whatever form seems to them to be fit for the purpose. However, the demands of summative assessment, with reliability to the fore, mean that there is a tendency for tutors to limit the range, form and length of responses, and for students to play safe by negotiating what sort of outcome is to be rewarded by the tutor (Becker, 1968). Summative assessment may co-exist with formative, but the price is that the formative side is severely compromised.

Chapter 2:

Some Principles for Sound Assessment

Characteristics of sound assessment

A paper from the UK Employment Department (1992) observes that a sound system, depending always on its purpose, will exhibit some, perhaps all, of the following characteristics:

- there will be clarity of purpose
- assessment will enable the learner to review progress and plan further learning
- similarly, it will allow the provider to review progress and adjudge teaching effectiveness
- it will be clear what is being assessed and how judgements are reached
- assessment will essentially assess what it claims to assess (validity)
- it will appear credible to tutors, learners and institutions
- it will be cost-efficient
- an outcome will be clear records of attainment which are useful to third parties
- the system itself will be subject to quality assurance procedures.

Objectively, though, sound assessment does not exist. It is far more useful to borrow the central idea of total quality management and talk about fitness for a purpose (Oakland, 1989). In this way we can see that formative assessment may have low reliability, but because it is the starting point in a discussion about development, and because it is regarded from the first as a tentative view, then this does not necessarily matter. There is a case for saying that in these circumstances a more reliable assessment would be inappropriate, being achieved at a greater cost, perhaps with some compromise to validity, and since it would appear to carry more authority it might inhibit the formative discussion by making the student passive in the face of authority.

Such 'fuzzy assessments' would be quite inappropriate in the certification of a professional pharmacist, or in the assessment of fitness to teach children, or in the award of a degree classification. The assessment should reflect certain standards, although these are often not well articulated, and be a reliable basis for saying whether the student has met those standards or not. We recognize that in practice those assessments are nothing like as reliable as they should be, but the principle remains. Later we will suggest that the simplest ways of swiftly improving the reliability of assessment are to:

- use more than one method to assess an achievement
- set more, albeit shorter, assessment items
- use more than one assessor (and one of the assessors may be the student-as-self-assessor, or another student).

Naturally, all things being equal, reliability is to be preferred over unreliability. Where reliability is defined as making accurate judgements of achievement against set criteria, as with NVQs, then it will generally be desirable, but since it is always bought at a cost, issues of audience and purpose cannot be escaped.

Multiple methods are best

Just as reliability is generally desirable but it is not always necessary to maximize it, so too there is no link between methods of assessment and the quality of assessment. Some universities have got into a rut, believing, for example, that history is about writing essays and that history students should therefore be assessed by essays. The best that can be said about this is that it is nonsense as a view of history and purblind as a response to the pressures on universities to demonstrate the breadth of their students' achievements. Multiple methods are necessary to assess multiple talents for multiple audiences.

Professional bodies typically demand that the practical competence of students be assessed, which might seem to constitute an exception to the rule that multiple methods are to be preferred. That is not the case, as Eraut and Cole (1993) have shown in their review of 12 professions. Even in management accounting, which used the fewest sources of evidence, four were used, students being assessed on the products of their normal professional work, on reflective reports, through log books and portfolios and by written examinations. Architecture used 10 out of the 11 assessment methods they identified. The assessment of practice is enriched by the use of multiple methods.This is a view which we hold despite evidence from the Quality in Higher Education (QHE) project that multiple assessment methods are not seen as a criterion of quality in HE (Harvey, 1993). They ought to be.

Multiple methods do carry problems with them. The main one is in weighting the scores produced by different methods, especially as one method may consistently produce a higher range of marks than another. This problem has hardly been addressed, although it is becoming noticeable in humanities subjects where marking is usually on an effective scale of 35–75. The assessment of oral presentations, which is often done by peer assessment when a checklist is filled in, rating presenters on five-point scales, seems to lead to a mark range of 50–90. The oral presentations skew the regular pattern. This presents a dilemma, for if oral skills are highly valued it would be disingenuous to give the oral work a weighting of, say, 5 per cent of the unit mark. On the other hand, there is no doubt that the two scales of marking are out of line. Heywood (1989) argues that the solution is to scale the oral marks so as to re-align them with the dominant scale. Thus a mark of 90 might come out at 74 and 50 might end up as 40.

Where multiple methods produce different messages about the same students, that is to say where the rank order differs quite seriously from one method to another, then the methods are assessing different sorts of achievement, all other things being equal. At this point there is no substitute for informed academic judgement about what the weightings ought to be on any one unit of assessment, always seeing this, as we shall argue, in the context of a department's whole assessment programme. Some institutions deal with this by separating courses from units of assessment. So, a learner may take three second-year sociology topics which lead to three different units of assessment, one on sociological theory, one on the substantive content of the two courses and one on oral communication skills.

Assessing multiple achievements

As fundamental to good assessment as the use of multiple methods is the assessment of multiple achievements. This is because a common characteristic of the HE curriculum is that it is to do with fostering complex and multi-faceted achievements. If that is the case, then following the logic that assessment shapes the actual curriculum and taking the line that HE institutions need to show how well student performance reflects their aims, sound assessment must be broad. By broad we mean not simply that a range of methods should be used, but that the range of *desiderata* must also be assessed. In the USA this has led to widespread activity to assess non-cognitive outcomes (Astin, 1991; Erwin, 1991; Lenning, 1988). The area is complex and it is far from clear that these summative assessments are either particularly reliable or valid. The effort is seen as worth making, though, because what employers seem to want to know most about graduates, assuming that some threshold of intellectual competence has been passed, is their personal and interpersonal qualities: the non-cognitive achievements during their undergraduate studies. How far it is possible to have a valid assessment of a person's commitment or leadership abilities is not clear, which is one reason why assessors have tended to concentrate on the cognitive areas of achievement.

Recent discussion of assessment has tended to overlook the fact that assessment is a moral activity. Someone chooses what is assessed: the desirable outcomes of HE are neither given, nor uncontentious, so neither is assessment.

In a recent study of the 'outcomes' approach to curriculum and assessment renewal, Otter (1992) showed that different stakeholders had different views of the outcomes which HE ought to foster (see also Harvey *et al.*, 1992). While the rhetoric of the times says that employers' views (and do employers speak with one voice?) ought to mould HE, whose purpose is to secure Britain's economic well-being, there are other views of the purposes of HE (see, for example, Atkins *et al.*, 1993). Selecting preferred outcomes – hence deciding what to assess – is not, therefore, a technical problem but a moral one.

The argument may be extended. The choice of assessment methods is also a moral choice. Copious assessment could be interpreted as hegemonic attempts to discipline and control. Likewise, certain methods reward certain types of learner. It is common to distinguish between 'deep' and 'surface' approaches to learning. This is a valuable distinction, as long as it is remembered that this, too, is not an 'all-or-nothing' distinction, although too much analysis not only acts as if it were, but also assumes that 'deep' learning is necessarily preferable to 'surface' learning. Our claim is that certain methods favour 'deep' learning approaches rather than 'surface' learning. The decision to prefer those methods is, then, a moral decision to favour students who conform to its requirements. Many overseas students, many 'A' level entrants, and mature students with notions of learning-as-fact-acquisition are devalued by such a decision.

Academics need to apply to assessment reform the same acuity that they apply to their own disciplines.

Fitness for purpose

At its simplest, as will be argued in Part 4, it is necessary for departments to match assessment methods to goals, as a basic exercise in checking the validity of what they ask students to do. Further scrutiny is needed when actual tasks are designed since there is quite a lot of evidence that the task as set – let alone the task as understood by the students – is often a low-level derivative of the task intended. So, students in initial teacher education might be told to write a 5,000-word explanation of how National Curriculum assessment arrangements might improve standards in primary schools. As presented, the task seems to get at writing and reference skills, to demand analysis and critical thinking. However, if the lecturer has already addressed this question in a lecture, the situation is very different, or if the reading includes a book called *Raising Standards Through the National Curriculum*, then again the actual task differs sharply from the ostensible task. The assessment system is not, in this case, sound, notably failing to deliver its promise. The failing is one of validity.

We shall, in Chapter 11, emphasize that assessment systems should produce data which are useful. Without that there is little point in assessing anyone. Since assessment data are at present scarcely used, it is easy to see why there is a certain scepticism about the need for assessment reform. One element of that reform is to insist that sound assessment is about using data as much as it is to do with collecting them.

This, in turn, means that the data must be fit for those purposes. Assessments need to produce usable data. For most purposes that means that they should produce informative data. What that means can be shown by comparing the typical report that a student got a 2:1 degree with a transcript saying what that student knew, understood and could do. The former produces data which is of use to virtually no one, although potential employers and research councils rely heavily on degree classifications. Even for the purpose of calculating how much progress students made during their undergraduate career this is a remarkably useless piece of information, for we would prefer to know what marks were gained for each unit (or better still how those marks arose out of different assessment tasks). The degree class says nothing about what the student had studied. Even were it to be accompanied by a transcript of courses and course grades, Adelman's study of practice in the USA shows that they are often opaque, unintelligible and plain unhelpful (Adelman, 1990).

Targeting assessment

In contrast, if assessments were targeted, so that students were assessed for whether they showed the ability to meet a given criterion for oral presentations, to take one example, then it would be possible to produce a 'can do' statement, although it would be more accurate to make it a 'has done' statement, since past performance is no guarantee of success in other circumstances. Information such as this is useful to all sorts of stakeholders. Most important, it is useful to the student. There is no reason why complex information such as this should not be simplified and reduced, if need be, to one grade. What is not acceptable is a situation where we really know little more about student achievements than the single grade expresses. This is painfully obvious when we look at university references and compare their unsupported generalities with the rich information which secondary schools, long accustomed to criterion-referenced assessment in the shape of GCSE, are able to provide on their 16-year-old leavers.

To summarize: sound assessments in HE:

- are valid, which means that they are related to the goals of universities, programmes and courses
- are targeted at multiple achievements
- use multiple methods
- assess the same 'outcomes' on several occasions (in medical training there might be 15 assessments of learners' ability to communicate with patients and 35–40 of medical diagnosis or problem-solving)

- produce useful and informative data
- are properly stored and well used within universities.

In the foregoing discussion it has been assumed that the unit of analysis is not the individual assessment activity but rather an assessment programme, say the set of assessment procedures associated with a Part II French programme. In that light we can add that sound assessments are:

- systemic – no assessment should be an island
- fit for the purpose.

So, the ideal system doesn't exist. The criteria for judging a system depend considerably on the perspective from which it is viewed (employer, student, manager) and on its purpose (ipsative, formative, summative). However, we have indicated certain features which are likely to recur in assessment systems which are fit for their purpose.

The message of this section is easily reduced to a phrase – there is a science of the art of assessment. The scientific aspects refer to the theories of reliability, to the idea of pre-testing assessment items, to establishing the facility and discriminatory power of questions, and to the processing and analysis of data. Largely drawn from psychometric schools of psychology, this science is a resource of considerable importance for some assessment purposes and should not be neglected. However, we shall not go very far into the details of these theories, referring readers to Anastasi (1988) and Heywood (1989).

The 'art' side refers to the way that matching techniques to programme goals and to the uses to which assessment data will be put is a matter for professional artistry. So too with devising assessment tasks, which can be as diverse as the imagination of the tutor, always given attention to validity and due thought as to reliability. Likewise, using assessment data may be subject to scientific analysis through a statistics package, or it may be the focus of sensitive discussion with a student for formative purposes. In the end it is the 'art' side which prevails, but it is foolish to stress the intuition of the individual professional to the detriment of all the social science knowledge about measuring human achievements, beliefs and attitudes.

The assessment of competence

The question of competence is inextricably linked with matters to do with criterion-referenced assessment. The notion of competence probably replaces, albeit at a more sophisticated level, the concept of skills. That doesn't necessarily make it easier to understand what competences (or skills, come to that) are, let alone how they are to be recognized. Just as it was hard to define what counted as a demonstration that a skill had been acquired or mastered, so too with competences. And as some (eg Pring, 1991) have argued, the idea of being competent in a professional role – as an engineer, accountant, nurse or teacher – is itself problematic, since competence in these fields involves expert behaviour which is not rule-bound and readily prescribed. As Pring put it, 'to be declared a competent teacher contains a mild criticism. One wants an imaginative, creative, intelligent, enthusiastic teacher too.' Someone may display the prescribed competences and still not be convincing as a practitioner, able to perform discrete actions but not able to integrate them convincingly.

Moreover, the competence approach often leads towards the specification of 'competences' in terms of outcomes that are remarkably like the discredited behavioural objectives, leading to lists which are 'too general, too bland, unrelated to specific analysis and unrelated to specific contexts' (*ibid.*); they also tend to be long lists. While competence is a pressing issue for the professions, it has wider ramifications, since universities need to be able to describe what any of their graduates know, understand and can do, and competences offers a means of doing that.

Winter (nd) has argued that professions are concerned with values, with emotional climates; that they have a store of experiential knowledge which is set in a rich knowledge context, and that this expertise is gained through principled reflection upon action. Drawing upon these integrating notions he has proposed a more convincing general model of professional competence which may be applied to the specifics of any one profession, avoiding the reductionism, positivism and atomization of the 'painting-by-numbers' style which characterizes attempts to specify what it means to be competent in more defined fields – as a telephonist or production operative, for example. Yet it does not dispose of the assessment problem. It may be possible to produce rather tighter accounts of competence in any given field, as the government persistently tries to do with school teaching (arguably, not very successfully). That does not do much to guide assessment.

The common line is that competence may be assessed by observation of practice (or a simulation of practice) and/or by the production of evidence which allows competence to be inferred. This is quite reasonable for any criterion-referenced assessment, but it neatly shows a problem for this approach, since criterion referencing carries with it the question of what would constitute a suitable demonstration of achievement. There is a sense in which this standard is specified in an arbitrary way, which raises the linked problems of how assessors are to be brought to agreement about the standard and how outsiders are to have confidence that the standard is reliably informed. It is undoubtedly better to have criteria than to have none, but this does not solve the problem of getting agreement amongst assessors – it simply displaces it.

A report (Gealy, 1993) of expert discussion of the assessment of competence and of knowledge concluded that there were problems in knowing how detailed expressions of standards should be. A notable problem lies in the idea that learners' knowledge might be assessed in order to make 'range statements', that is, estimates of the range of circumstances in which the designated competence might be expected to be displayed.

This has been offered as a neat compromise between those who want to see knowledge assessed and those who want to see competence assessed. Gealy noted that the underlying professional or subject knowledge base does need to be specified, since otherwise it 'can lead to enormous variation in what assessors and course designers assume to be required' (p.6). However, it remains unclear how much knowledge ought to be assessed, and in what conditions, in order to make what types of 'range statements'. The solution has an air of meretriciousness about it. However, there is no reason to disagree with the conclusion that 'the demands of assessment at higher levels may require greater imagination and new ways of working' (p.7).

One thing seems to be quite clear, which is that a case begins to emerge for working towards agreements amongst HE institutions about the criteria and standards to be applied. One avenue for this is through subject associations, such as the Engineering Professors' Conference (EPC, 1992). Another is through regional collaboration amongst universities, which may well be encouraged through modularization and the development of Credit Accumulation and Transfer (CATs) conventions. A third way is through thorough-going reform of the system of external examiners. Some say that a fourth way may prove to be the emergence of a core national curriculum for HE.

Chapter 3:

Purposes of Assessment

Criticisms of assessment

Assessment is a complex business. Why bother? Surely hardly assessing students, perhaps only through finals examinations, has powerful advantages? We reject that point of view, but it would be wrong not to consider it seriously. Having done that we shall outline problems with the criticisms and turn to our view that assessment is for learning. Criticisms first. If we assess infrequently and lightly:

- it frees learners from the treadmill of continuous coursework, allowing them to read around the subject
- consequently, it allows them to experiment and to play with ideas, to explore unpromising avenues and to follow intellectual curiosity
- this would be more 'life-like' – after all, academics are not regularly assessed in this form. An academic article is the product of time, thought, research, reading and interest, has been through several drafts and has probably been enriched by peer criticism
- continuous assessment leads to a regression to the mean – put another way, it is hard to sustain a first-class standard over many pieces of assessed work, easier to do so over fewer pieces
- it encourages 'surface' approaches to learning. A not-too-clear distinction has been drawn between 'deep' and' surface' approaches to learning. Essentially 'surface' approaches involve memorization and reproduction above all. Learning theory says that understanding is not a prominent characteristic of these approaches, since understanding involves the act of reconciling the new information with existing knowledge. 'Surface' learning is seen as relatively passive. 'Deep' learning, on the other hand, involves a quest for understanding and involves an interaction with the new information, which is substantially reworked in the learning

process. It has been said that this information will then be better remembered and that the learner will be more able to use and apply it, to evaluate its strengths and weaknesses and to see directions for further learning. 'Deep' learning is seen as an important goal of HE. *Excessive assessment*, especially where the assessments are clichéd, leads students to adopt surface learning as a coping strategy

- it puts a premium on coverage of content at the expense of depth of understanding – superficial acquaintance is encouraged
- assessments are often unreliable, hence arbitrary, and the range of assessment techniques which any student encounters is likely to be equally arbitrary
- it is therefore counter-educational, fostering extrinsic motivation and dependency; discouraging self-assessment, responsibility and initiative; empowering lecturers, not students
- it wastes an enormous amount of staff time
- there are fears that the fiasco of National Curriculum assessment in schools may be exported to HE, using up scarce time, constraining the curriculum, encouraging didactic teaching, and leading to a bureaucratic jamboree of paperwork
- it produces seemingly 'hard' data about student performance which are used as performance indicators, when in fact the data, coming from frequently invalid measures, and being an excessively simplified description of the results, are of very little value
- because the system is 'comfy' and appears to work, it conceals the importance of thinking intelligently about the whole business of learning and teaching, perpetuating nineteenth-century practices as we enter the twenty-first century.

The case is, then, that the present system (or lack of a system!) is essentially flawed, and that there are good grounds for preferring little, if any, assessment to what we have at present.

Criticising the criticisms

Requiring fewer items of assessed work would meet the objection of regression to the mean and also tackle the overload issue. Some tutors might suspect that fewer assessed items would lead to less work being done by basically idle students. A solution which also has the advantages of allowing students to experiment, and of making it easy to introduce some form of peer- and self-assessment, is to require work to be done but to insist that findings be presented in a concise form and to make the work qualificatory, not graded. This system operates in the second year of the BA/QTS teacher education programme at S. Martin's College, Lancaster, and colleagues tell us that the students do the work and they do it well. Such an approach would also cut the burden of marking on tutors. Moreover, with less to be assessed, students could be encouraged to get 'under the skin' of the topics which they do prepare for assessment, and 'deep' approaches to learning would be implicated in their doing so.

Hand-in-hand with this goes the need to reconsider the work which we ask students to do for assessment. There is no doubt that there is an enormous inertia attached to the present system, which tends to reward comparatively low-level activities, to disempower the student and to demand the demonstration of a lopsided set of achievements. This, we argue, is largely the case because assessment and, indeed, the curriculum have not been thought about hard enough nor consistently enough. The criticisms that 'surface' learning is encouraged, that a narrow range of assessment techniques is used, that students' achievements are poorly documented and that assessment practices discourage thought about learning and teaching are not criticisms which are automatically attached to the business of assessment. They are largely the result of indifference to the issues, reinforced by tradition and complacency.

The complaint that assessment results are rather arbitrary needs to be taken more seriously, since the solutions are not quite so simple. Of course, if the assessment is formative and contributes to a dialogue between students and tutors, then the inaccuracies may not matter too much, since the assessment is simply a starting bid in a process of trying to identify areas for development and areas of competence. However, where the assessment is summative and carries with it the awful verdict that this person has a second-class mind, then it is important to minimize assessment error. We have commented upon the importance of having clear criteria, of using reliable *processes* of assessment and of setting more but shorter and more sharply targeted items. Reform of the external examiner system is certainly needed.

To this list may be added the old chestnuts of anonymous marking (assessors are supposed not to know whose work is being assessed), double marking, and unseen double marking, where the second assessor is ignorant of the mark suggested by the first. In our view students' common requests for such reforms are not always well-conceived. Anonymous marking and formative assessment hardly go well together, while unseen double marking is difficult unless the second marker is as expert in the field as the first, which is not common. There is some evidence that double marking actually narrows the range of marks awarded. We suggest that there is no substitute for increasing reliability by making criteria clear and involving students in the assessment process.

Hitherto we have not addressed the question, 'Why assess?' so much as explained why common criticisms of assessment are not to be taken at face value. There are, we believe, very positive reasons for assessing students. Some of them have been mentioned in the section on motives for assessment, but it is worth drawing together the possible benefits of assessment at this point.

Assessment for learning – by students, staff and systems

Why, then, do we assess? There are many reasons why assessment has become an integral part of academic practice, many of them valid and creditable and others perhaps more dubious. This section examines more closely why we do it, so that the assessment we choose to undertake can be done for sound and expedient reasons.

Students expect it

Most students in HE have at least ten years of formal education behind them, and assessment has usually formed a considerable part of this process. Throughout schooling students have had their energies regulated and learning activities punctuated by assessment, and they expect tertiary education to be much the same. Often the hardest part of working for a higher degree, such as a Masters degree by research, is the lack of interim assessment that many students get used to having earlier in their academic career. It is normally more helpful to have staged or continuous assessment on any learning project to help keep up momentum.

Students are motivated by assessment

Often the first question students ask is whether a course is to be assessed and they vote with their feet in unassessed components. In recent years students have become much more strategic in their study patterns, rarely studying for the love of learning alone, but concentrating their energies on what will get them a better degree or a higher project mark.

This means that getting them to accept the value of formative assessment will not be simple, and that if formative assessment is not inbuilt as a normal, natural procedure in all courses, then its effects are likely to be severely compromised by this extrinsic, mark-driven motivation.

Although students complain about having to complete assignments, studying can be a disheartening experience without assessment. If students do not know how they are doing, they tend to stop working, unless their internal motivation is very high. Motivation and feedback are therefore intertwined.

It can provide feedback

One of the most common complaints students make is about unmarked assignments. They can become very dissatisfied when they put a lot of energy into completing assessment tasks, which then seem to be ignored by the tutor. They tend to express views subsequently that there is no point in doing further assignments because they never get their work back. We return later to the importance of feedback.

Receiving feedback can be an excellent motivator, especially when valid criticism is supported by appropriate praise and commentary. However, it is not always easy to provide the level and depth of feedback that one would desire, especially when there are large numbers of students. We provide some suggestions on how to deal with this problem in Chapter 8.

One of the commonest forms of assessment in HE, examinations, normally provides no feedback at all, apart from a final grade. Exams are widely used because they are cost-effective, easy to administer and usually thought to be objective and fair. They do not generally provide any formative information for students at all on how to improve, simply a summative result, indicating an end result, usually a number, that the student has to interpret as best as he or she can.

As an opportunity for student learning, exams are normally empty, simply recording achievement. There will be occasions when this is appropriate, perhaps, for example, at the very end of a learning process, but these occasions are much less common, we would assert, than is often believed to be the case.

It can help students remedy mistakes

If students do not get feedback, they may continue to make the same mistakes repeatedly and fail to improve performance. Learning should not be a guessing game in which students have to estimate what might be in a tutor's mind and then perform accordingly. They should be clear about the demands of assignments so that they have every chance to achieve well. However, it is not desirable to set over-prescribed tasks with little, if any, opportunity to demonstrate individuality or creativity. They also need clear guidance as to what they might have done better in assignment tasks, so that they can do it next time, and so that they learn appropriate material for examinations and for application beyond the learning environment.

It helps with option choice and selection

It is useful for students to have information on option choices which can be provided by appropriate assessment tasks. Where, for example, students must decide whether to take French or German as the major second-year subject in a languages degree, it is helpful for them to have some kind of external indicator of their own performance, rather than relying on personal preference or gut reaction. Indeed, if a student then goes on to choose the option that assessment suggests is his or her weaker subject, at least this is an informed choice.

Similarly, where the tutor is the person who makes the choice about individual students' option routes, assessments will to some extent provide guidance that does not rely on subjectivity or guesswork.

It indicates readiness for progression

Where progression depends on competence, for example, when students are not deemed ready to progress to the next stage of learning a language until they have achieved a good level of ability at a lower stage, then assessment can be helpful in providing guidance. This can be oriented towards the learners' needs, as is often the case in computer-based tutorials, when satisfactory completion of an assessment task is necessary before a student is advised to move on to the next learning unit.

It can also be tutor-driven, with the tutor guiding the student towards appropriate levels of study, into a more rapidly working group, for example, or into remedial or equalization sessions.

It can help diagnose faults

Students can be guided when they are doing things badly or incorrectly by the feedback we give them on their work. This is often one of the more valued aspects of a tutor's role, when students are given fairly detailed comments, in writing or orally, about what is going wrong, so that they do not continue to make the same mistakes. Students tend to concentrate their energies where these will have best effect. Obviously, they prefer to get things right, but when they do not do so, they like to know where they have gone wrong, so that they don't do it again.

It provides a performance indicator for students

In looking at a batch of work, we can usually determine how well students are doing in relation to one another (normative feedback) and how well they are doing in relation to their earlier work (ipsative feedback). The type of feedback given will depend on the purpose and the nature of the assignment set.

It enables grading and final degree classification

In HE we are normally expected to make qualitative decisions about the levels of achievement our students attain, and assessment enables us to do this. No one would expect to decide a final-year students' degree classification simply on hunch or a subjective response, so assessment of some kind will be necessary. However, we will repeatedly insist that it is vital to avoid an over-reliance on any one single method of assessment – exams, for example – as all forms of assessment disadvantage some students. It is normally advisable, therefore, to use a varied repertoire of assessment methods which can give a more valid and reliable picture of a student's ability than reliance on a single methodology can.

It provides a performance indicator for staff

If one or two students do badly in an assignment, we can usually assume it is the students who need attention, but where a whole cohort hands in inadequate or incorrect work, this indicates some kind of failure in the teaching or assignment briefing methodologies. We then have fairly firm indicators that something needs to be changed, and often some hints on how we should do so.

Some staff may choose to use student results as an indicator of their own excellence as a teacher during their appraisal or in negotiations for promotion or additional performance-related pay. However, we should avoid excessive reliance on results as an indicator of the excellence (or the reverse) of a lecturer, because other factors such as the quality of the intake and the resource base of the learning environment can have as much effect on results as the quality of the teaching itself. This is further discussed in Chapters 11 and 12.

It provides a performance indicator for the course and the institution

Increasingly institutions are going to be required to provide evidence of quality, and a readily measurable performance indicator is student performance as shown through assignment and exam results. In former polytechnics, academics were habituated to having to account for results in course review or quality audit procedures, and many of the older universities had established good practice in this area.

As we shall show in Chapter 11, assessment data are important for the effective operation of course development and review and for total quality management systems, all of which depend upon information about present performance as well as about ambitions for future performance.

We have always done it

Often academics set assessment tasks because we know it is expected of us, rather than because we have clearly thought out reasons for doing so. Indeed, as we have indicated, there are excellent reasons why assessment must form a part of the learning and teaching processes. But, just as students study strategically, so too we should assess strategically, devoting our energies to the most efficient and effective types of assessment for our purposes. All too often we set tasks of the type, duration and scope that we or our predecessors have done for years, rather than thinking through what we expect the outcomes of those assignments might be. This again is an area to be addressed in Chapter 10.

Assessment is learning

The only questions that matter are who assesses, what and how. The idea of learning without some form of assessment of what has been learned is inconceivable. The assessment may be self-assessment and come later, as when we think we know how to fix a leaky tap and find that we don't. It may be self-assessment and be on the spot, as when you read something and mutter that you don't understand what it's getting at. It may be peer assessment, as when colleagues say that your last publication was a 'serviceable guide to the older literature'. Whatever, feedback, evaluation, judgement and assessment are inherent in learning and living. And necessary for both.

Theories of assessment

It is not enough to appreciate that assessment can have enormous value as a tool for learning, and that it provides important data for review, management and planning. It needs to be shown *how* assessment is supposed to do this, *how* weighing the pig can fatten it. Just as we would need a theory of porcine growth to explain the logic of weighing pigs, so too we need a theory of assessment – or theories, because different assessment purposes require different theories.

We will distinguish between a theory of summative assessment and a theory of formative assessment, while recognizing that a less crude distinction (which we commended earlier) would lead to a greater number of more subtle theories. Following that we shall examine the theoretical relationship between assessment and institutional change.

A theory of summative assessment

In *summative assessment* there is a disjuncture between the theory as it should be and the theory-in-use. As it should be, the theory says that summative assessment represents a valid and reliable sampling of student achievements, which leads to a meaningful statement of what they know, understand and can do. Employers and admissions tutors are able to use this information as the basis for their decisions, although, since the work or continuing education environment will differ in crucial respects from the undergraduate experience, interviews and perhaps some further assessment are likely to complement universities' summative assessments. Tests of this theory's power would include whether employers do rely on universities' assessments and whether these assessments have predictive validity, which is to say whether student grades align well with their success in their working careers. Unfortunately, the evidence is that employers are not influenced in detail by summative assessments and that there is not a strong correlation between degree class and earning power (Tarsh, 1990).

The theory-in-use seems to be that employers recognize that assessments are not especially reliable and they know that what is reported is usually just a slice of students' achievements. They seem to treat degree class as a threshold variable, deciding that anyone with a 2:1, for example, has the potential to do the job. The characteristics which then interest them are ones not well described by existing summative accounts: characteristics such as flexibility, the ability to work in a team, the potential to lead a team, initiative, reliability, motivation, interpersonal skills and so on. Employers, then, find themselves having to make their own assessments of these things, often in a fairly haphazard way. Notice that the degree is being taken as little more than a talisman, as evidence that the student is a person with some intellectual standing who has undergone a rite of passage. It is quite common for employers to say that they are happy to recruit graduates from many disciplines, the subject of undergraduate study being irrelevant to the detailed demands of the job. This is even the case when a student who has studied psychology goes into a job requiring a psychology degree, for the psychology he or she will need is likely to be quite different from the psychology that he or she knows, with the psychological way of thinking being perhaps the only bridge between undergraduate studies and work.

On this simple theory of summative assessment, that it is providing information for the postgraduate employment and education system, we have to conclude that present assessment procedures are inadequate. They seem designed to tell only university academics anything, and in any case it is doubtful, as we shall say in Part 4, whether they use assessment data to any good purpose.

A theory of formative assessment

A theory of *formative assessment* is much more complicated and tentative. It depends upon assumptions about the student, the task and the tutor. These assumptions clarify the type of learning environment which we should try to construct if we want to make formative learning powerful. And let us be clear that we believe that this is vital, on two grounds. First, formative learning has the implication that growth is to be promoted, not left to the swirling patterns of 'natural' development by exposure to the subject matter of the degree. Second, we believe that formative learning provides a model for self-directed learning and hence for intellectual autonomy. Where students start by negotiating with tutors about areas of strength and of weakness, they are increasingly encouraged to be more autonomous in appraising their performances, learning to be reflective and to take responsibility for their own growth. From assessment as something done to students, we move to assessment as something done with students and thence to assessment as something done for students. This is the path to the professionalism which is the model of HE.

The assumptions about the students are:

- that they are motivated to learn
- intrinsic motivation exists, although extrinsic motivation (being driven by praise, other rewards and by fear of failure) will do. However, extrinsic motivation is rather limited, since students will have to get their rewards from far more complex responses to their work than a simple percentage mark would indicate: it will be quite common for there not to be a mark given to a piece of formative work
- they take seriously the business of weighing their work against the available criteria. This means that students and staff share goals and that they share understandings of what those goals mean. We are not saying

that they need to share behavioural objectives, but that they need to have a shared view of where they might be going
- they take seriously the business of weighing others' work against those criteria
- they use their insights when discussing their work with tutors or with their academic counsellors
- feedback is rapid and appropriately timed so that it can be used formatively
- they act on the basis of the feedback which they have given themselves and had from others while doing the work and on the basis of the completed task
- they continue to use this feedback, especially to shape later pieces of work
- hence, they can handle the ambiguity and complexity of criterion-referenced assessment, taking an ipsative, rather than a norm-referenced, approach.

While we have insisted that assessment methods are neutral, in the sense of being neither formative nor summative, it is evident that the tasks set need to be carefully devised if the formative function is to succeed. This is an organizational matter which is not related to the choice of any particular assessment technique. Tasks should:

- be such that full feedback is generated for the students' use. That feedback will often come from academics, but it will sometimes come from peers, and increasingly it should come from the student, given the goal of encouraging a reflective cast of mind
- have criteria for successful completion available. These criteria may come from the tutor, but they may also come from peers, and increasingly they should be shaped by the student. A common practice is for some of the criteria to be prescribed by the tutors or the department, while others are provided by the students or jointly agreed
- direct students' attention to the importance of drawing upon earlier experiences of this sort of activity, or to previous encounters with this type of subject matter, situation or problem: the habit of using feedback needs to be over-taught
- ideally, have review points built in where students have to pause and either reflect themselves upon what they are doing and what they know about how to do the task, or sound out colleagues or tutors
- be achievable, which is to say that they should be matched to students' existing or *emerging competences*. That also means that the assessment should be valid
- reflect the goals of the curriculum – if students can complete tasks by doing less than the curriculum intends that they should, then they will. Poorly devised tasks produce a stunted operational curriculum.

Tutors' jobs therefore become much more complicated, which is why we insist that assessment reform depends upon teaching being given a greater priority in universities. That is not quite the same as saying that assessment will take up more time, since some of the methods described in Part 2 can save time and we argue in Chapter 11 that a well devised assessment *system* does save time in the medium and long terms. It does mean that tutors will need to respond to work with more careful thought about the task and about the individual student who has done it. That in turn implies that tasks will have to be more purposefully conceived than has been commonplace. Tutors will need to:

- give full feedback, when they are the assessor, rather than the student or peers, which is related both to the criteria for successful completion and to the individual student (problems posed by modularization are discussed in Part 4)
- identify with students points for development
- set or agree tasks which embody a broad and balanced curriculum (see Part 4)
- generate and share criteria which blend departmental requirements with student priorities
- grade rapidly – effective feedback is swift feedback
- see the job as empowering students, hence see it as principally a counselling and facilitating job
- be aware of the best thinking on student learning in HE
- be supportive, foster intrinsic motivation, preferably by being interesting and enthusiastic.

There are two major implications of formative assessment for the university as a whole:

- students need to have academic counsellors who periodically meet them, review progress across the whole programme, identify areas for further attention, while having in mind possible career paths and relevant personal circumstances
- teaching has to be given greater priority, and with it training for teaching which is in harmony with formative assessment.

The products of formative assessment may never show up in the form of grades on a record sheet. Ungrading, where work is commented upon but where no mark is attached, may become the norm, freeing up the assessment system by allowing experiment and risk-taking. We are not saying that students ought not to get feedback: on the contrary. It might be that qualitative and formative feedback has scope which is denied quantitative and summative assessment methods. For those worried that this could mean that too little summative assessment data might be produced: there could be provision for students to compile a portfolio of the most interesting pieces of work, accompanied by a 1000-word commentary, which could be used by boards of examiners as supplementary evidence.

Again, this theory shows how much needs to be done with our current system. Astin (1991,p.189) was certain that 'the best principles of assessment and feedback are seldom followed or applied in the typical lower-division undergraduate course'. At its simplest, it seems that there is little scope for formative assessment because too many assessments (examinations stand out here) do not lead to feedback to the students. There is also dissatisfaction with the quality of feedback which students often get, and there is a shortage of research into the way that students use – or are required to use – the feedback which they do get. A major improvement in assessment systems would be to examine carefully departmental policies for generating feedback to students.

Notice that the theory of formative assessment is close to being a theory of learning. Certainly, assessment is being used to shape and direct future learning. In helping students to a conscious knowledge of what they know, understand and can do, it is developing metacognition, which is being identified as a key component in successful learning. Metacognitive thinkers are aware of the strategies available to them and are able to select the best for a particular situation, behaving, thereby, as deep learners. Surface learning is more characteristic of learners who plough into problems without thinking about the material: they behave as though the goal were to reproduce what they have noted, to duplicate, not to create understanding.

Assessment and institutions

One further theory of assessment needs to be mentioned in this setting. *How is assessment to contribute to institutional management?* Often neglected, this aspect of assessment is crucial: Erwin (1991, p.119) said that 'for the typical faculty [lecturer] or student affairs staff member, the major value of assessment is to improve existing programmes'. He might have gone further and said that in a learning organization assessment data are the engine of change in the same way as profit maximization directs the activities of commercial corporations. We dwell upon this in Part 4.

Chapter 4:

Forces for Change

Students' views

People go to university for many reasons, not all of which are to do with academic success. However, most wish to do well – that is, to get a good degree – and most hope that they will get an acceptable job with their good degree. Since it is they who are assessed, perhaps they should be asked how it is to be done. They may answer that this is for employers and academics to decide, or go to the other extreme and say that they would prefer not to be assessed. Whatever, the mood of the times is such that the stakeholders should be asked.

We report on a study done at Lancaster and on two larger-scale ones before turning to a second Lancaster study of feedback to students.

Lancaster University, assessment and examinations, 1993

University-wide issues identified by Baldwin (1993) included: why do we have examinations? Why is the assessment formula as it is? What skills am I being assessed on? Third-year students in one academic department – 98 of them – were closely questioned about assessment.

Assessment items were seen to be about the right length, but there was criticism of the bunching of items: like London buses, coursework pieces all come together. (The same was said of examinations.) Twenty-two per cent said that assessment is relevant to the goals of the course. Most (67 per cent) said that it was 'more or less' relevant and 11 per cent denied any relevance to course goals. Yet one of the most common comments was that course objectives were not always clear, that criteria for assessment were unclear, and there was a sense in the open-ended responses that assessment was a game of giving tutors what they wanted – and that tutors differed, with the result that assessment was not so much about demonstrating commonly-held competence but getting the measure of individual assessors. 'I wrote what I thought the tutors wanted', said one respondent. Such comments remind us that what tutors see from the point of view of *their* course, students see in a holistic fashion, looking for consistency and coherence in the practices and standards of *all* the tutors they encounter; and students may meet many tutors – too many?

Unsurprisingly, 87 per cent said that marking varied from tutor to tutor. Six per cent of students were clear about the marking criteria, 44 per cent were vaguely aware of the criteria to be used and 50 per cent were unclear.

Exams were almost universally disliked, characterized as exercises in cramming of an invalid sort, scarcely appropriate to a programme of professional education. Their summative nature was criticized: if exams are to be set, then it might be useful to spread them more evenly across the programme and ensure that feedback gave year 1–3 exams a formative as well as a summative function. Given that exams have to be done, two-thirds of these third-years thought the number of exams (*not* their timing) was acceptable.

The Quality in HE Project, University of Central England, 1992

Questions were asked of eight 'stakeholding' groups, including employers, students and staff in HE. Forty-three criteria of quality HE are listed in the *Executive Summary* (Harvey *et al.*, 1992). Students and staff were agreed that of importance were that 'assessment is valid, objective and fair', 'assessment criteria are clear and understood by staff and students', 'assessment covers the full range of course aims and objectives' and 'students receive useful feedback from assessment (and are kept informed of progress)'. The interesting question is to what extent these criteria (which were *not* of much interest to employers, who seemed to prefer to ensure quality by liaison over the nature of provision) are being met by universities.

London University's 'Identifying and developing a quality ethos for teaching in Higher Education' study, 1993

This study from CHES (Williams, 1993) sheds some light on the degree to which a different sample of students, academics and administrators/ managers thought certain characteristics of effective teaching to be present in universities. One of the five characteristics of effective lecturers which students thought were often insufficiently in evidence was providing prompt and detailed feedback. Lecturers and administrators both included it too in their list of areas of shortfall.

Academics looked to see communication skills, creativity and problem-solving skills developed, with students agreeing to the first two of these and employers ranking them first, second and fifth. The point here is that these, and the desirable commitment to lifelong learning mentioned by academics, are affected by the way students are assessed. Given the report of shortfalls, we may infer that assessment programmes are seen to fail in these areas. The fact that assessment programmes are not mentioned in the 'aspects of institutional culture that contribute to effective teaching' rather supports that interpretation.

Feedback to Lancaster students

Turner (1993) interviewed some 20 undergraduates on the nature and quality of the feedback which they got from tutors. In many ways his findings confirm the CHES observation and earlier Lancaster work which had shown the variable, often negative quality of written feedback to students. His in-depth interview methods helped to bring out that students do differ in what they want by way of feedback: not too much, said some; more, said others. The main conclusion is that where written feedback is legible it is not always helpful. However, we have argued that formative assessment stands or falls on the quality of feedback. Findings such as Turner's give, therefore, cause for concern.

Summary

These studies neatly show why we should never be too committed to any one method of assessing, since different research methods and questions have produced rather different results. Let us suggest five ways of reading these findings.

First, students do want to be assessed fairly and broadly. The list of course characteristics which students in the CHES study said should be more emphasized would support that opinion.

Second, they want prompt feedback. That may not mean that tutors have to write copious comments at high speed. If we take the QHE point, it may be more important for these comments to be clearly related to agreed criteria. Some of the CHES findings which we have not reported here support that. Lancaster data indicate that tutors may not have got a grip on giving 'useful' feedback.

Third, there is the relative absence of an emphasis on examinations.

Fourth, students do not speak with one voice, nor should we expect that. If we might categorize them into those whose approaches to learning are variously 'deep', 'surface', 'strategic' and 'apathetic', then it follows that certain assessment methods are likely to sit better with some approaches than others. Moreover, there are probably variations between students taking different subjects.

Fifth, notice how little assessment is a live concern. Yet our claim is that unless assessment is reformed, the curriculum cannot be. And the CHES and QHE findings, let alone the force of the Employment Department, politicians and others, say that the curriculum must be reformed to provide HE fit for the millennium.

Other catalysts for change

The main reason why assessment has to change is that the curriculum is having to change. Two aspects of that change are noteworthy here, and both will only happen if assessment systems are designed to abet them.

One face of change is the need, expressed in the CHES study, to ensure that students encounter, as of right, programmes intended to advance a good collection of achievements. Over recent years Enterprise in Higher Education (EHE) has been a great force for this.

Developments in the way professional learning is being conceived (Winter, nd) and the exercises to develop NVQs at Level 5 take us down the same route. Not only do they start from a notion of what we want students in a certain category to master, but they then insist that if it's important enough to be on the list, then it should be assessed. Simultaneously they represent a broadening – *in certain senses* – of the curriculum, and they power the move to criteria-referenced, competence-led assessments.

Some employers are supportive of this, although the QHE data implied that the way students are assessed is of less current concern than how the curriculum is constructed. Where employers are increasingly involved in workplace-based learning and assessment, as is the case with nursing, social work, teaching and tailor-made programmes, employers are more involved in assessment issues, often coming to realize how complex and costly they can be.

The second face is the need to change the curriculum to handle the growth in student numbers without corresponding growth in staff, buildings and other resources. Cheaper ways of teaching have to be found, which is curriculum change of a compelling kind. Few cheaper ways will be found if assessment methods remain predicated upon former assumptions about teaching, let alone about learning. It may well be that cheaper methods deal in the language of empowering students. If that is so, congruence demands that assessment should do likewise. Besides, on many courses it is assessment which ties tutors down – and often they would be happier researching, reading or preparing, which means that assessment *feels* more wearisome.

Interest has been shown in increasing student numbers by recruiting from groups who have not traditionally participated heavily in HE. Access courses have often been innovative in their assessment, but here we wish to concentrate upon the Accreditation of Prior Experience and Learning (APEL). At its simplest this means that some students will get their degree without going through the same university assessment programme as most other entrants. It should be recognized that some professionals almost routinely get APEL credit for having worked at a professional level for so many years. Undoubtedly this pushes universities to consider what such students should know and demonstrate, and how. Some would argue that the whole meaning of a degree is being altered by these developments: certainly fundamental assumptions are being re-examined.

The last force for change in assessment practices which we will mention is technological. Information technology supports self-assessment and expert systems (Gentle, 1992), as well as accelerating marking multiple choice tests.

Conclusions and concern

Assessment is basic to learning: to students' learning; to academics' learning about becoming better teachers and facilitators; to systems' learning about what they are doing well and less well. A simple Venn diagram in Figure 4.1 shows our view of the relationship.

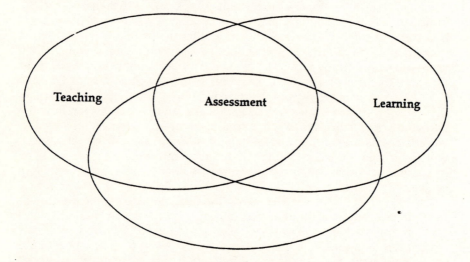

Figure 4.1 *Assessment, teaching and learning*

It is equally important for development, notably for universities' development of programmes as well as their development of human potential. So far from it being the case that you'll not fatten a pig by weighing it, we have said that the science of weighing is necessary for the art of development.

Unfortunately, while there are plenty of current concerns about the assessment system, one matter of considerable importance is that those concerns are not more widely shared. Assessment is still not the high-profile issue which it should be, given the argument that it is assessment arrangements which determine the curriculum in action. This can be illustrated by looking at the reports of the Academic Audit Unit (AAU). A review of 23 of the 27 audit reports related to visits done between March 1991 and June 1992 found that very little was said about universities' assessment systems.

Such comments as there were in the AAU reports tended to amount to an observation that assessment arrangements were considered by faculties at the course proposal or course/departmental review stage. This did not mean that assessment was considered in terms of the course aims and objectives: at Exeter, exceptionally, codes of good teaching practice are to 'address the question of what methods of assessment best suit the various objectives of courses and programmes of study'; at Salford, departmental teaching and learning committees are expected to consider 'methods of assessment of students consistent with the course objectives'. However, more common were references to discussions about whether students' work should be double- and anonymously marked.

Further evidence that assessment has not been addressed seriously comes from the reports that practices and standards diverge sharply *within* universities, which causes particular problems for students on combined degree schemes. At Durham, the audit team drew

attention to the confusions which can result from the use of too great a range of assessment conventions, especially in the case of joint honours, combined studies and some other . . . programmes. Students . . . expressed uncertainty about the arrangements for, and the criteria used in, their assessment.

At York, auditors spoke of 'the desirability of co-ordinating and monitoring assessment practices throughout the University'. The report on Essex noted that

it seemed doubtful whether the University itself was in a position to provide full information on the range of departmental assessment practices currently being used, and this suggested that it was important that the University should consider developing ways of monitoring assessment practices generally.

At Loughborough, 'assessment and marking practice . . . vary across the University; these are questions likely to receive continued attention, not least from the students'. At Sheffield, 'staff to whom the audit team spoke did appear to wish for greater central guidance [on assessment practice]'.

At Strathclyde, assessment data were being used inappropriately as performance indicators and, overall, there were few references to consideration of – let alone innovation in – assessment practices. Exeter's staff development day on assessment was exceptional. We also note that the PCFC-funded *Teaching Large Groups Project* did take assessment seriously enough to run training days and to produce a pamphlet on assessing large groups.

Yet, we maintain that concern over assessment is not rampant. And that is the biggest concern of all for us, since we believe that assessment reform is to be the key issue in university development in the UK.

It is to techniques of weighing and to the attendant process of promoting learning that we now turn.

Part 2: Assessment methods

It does rather look as though my Council of Europe work will cut into the beginning of the autumn term, so I wonder if you'd be an angel and explain the basic principles of self-teaching to my four first year groups, and if that doesn't keep them quiet, offer a guaranteed B+ to the longest essay irrespective of merit (Postcard from Dr Piercemuller to departmental secretary, as reported by Laurie Taylor in *The Times Higher Education Supplement*, 27 August 1993).

Assessment will be seen as natural and helpful, rather than threatening and sometimes a distraction from real learning as in traditional models (Jessup, 1991, p.136).

Chapter 5:

Dimensions of Assessment

We repeat that assessment techniques work best where learning outcomes have been articulated in advance, shared with students and assessment criteria agreed. Questions about the purpose of assessment necessarily arise, especially questions related to formative as opposed to summative purposes. Assessment techniques which are integrated into the course, not 'bolted-on' are desirable – this implies both staff and curriculum development. Moreover, it may be that some techniques are best suited to pass/fail assessment, not lending themselves to the fine distinctions which go with concepts of unit grades. Finally, it is increasingly debatable who should be doing the assessing, with there being a considerable interest in students assessing – and advising – each other and themselves; this is closely related to the negotiation between staff and students of learning outcomes and activities. A significant part of this is self- and peer assessment, and it is there that we start our review of assessment methods.

Self-assessment

Developing students' own judgement

There are numerous reasons why students should be involved in assessing their own work. In the first instance, students will be expected to practise self-evaluation in every area of their lives on graduation, and it is a good exercise in self-development to ensure that these abilities are extended. In many of the types of assessment that students undertake, they are expected to assess *process* as well as *product*, and while the assessment of product is very often best undertaken by a third person, assessment of process necessarily involves those involved in that process. Where, for example, students are being assessed in groups, it is essential that if the process of group working is to be assessed, the participants themselves should be involved in so doing.

Self- and peer assessment give learners a greater ownership of the learning they are undertaking. Assessment is not then a process done to them, but is a participative process in which they are themselves involved. This in turn tends to motivate students, who feel they have a greater investment in what they are doing.

Using self- and peer assessment makes the process much more one of learning because learners are able to share with one another the experiences that they have undertaken. Too often assessment is a private process between tutor and student where the learning and experiences of the student have no wider audience than the tutor, who will tend to see so many examples that it will not add to the general base of knowledge available. For peer assessment, especially, ideas can be interchanged and effective learning will take place. Students will become more experienced at learning and will become more autonomous learners, able to stand on their own feet without the kind of passive dependence on the tutor for information and assessment that has been traditionally the case in much of HE.

Self- and peer assessment enable learners to develop their own transferable personal skills in such areas as group work, leadership, teamwork, creative thinking and problem-solving.

Self-evaluation and evaluation of the contribution of one's peers are not skills which are lightly undertaken, and are not skills that can be undertaken without a certain amount of training. Students will need a great deal of practice in preparation for self- and peer assessment; they cannot just be thrown in at the deep end.

Self-assessment and self-grading

There is a big difference between self-assessment and self-grading. Self-assessment involves the use of evaluative processes in which judgement is involved, where self-grading is the marking of one's own work against a set of criteria and potential outcomes provided by a third person, usually the tutor.

Self- and peer grading have been undertaken widely throughout the years and have a part to play in informal and unimportant assessment processes; but self- and peer assessment as evaluative tools should be used to a much greater extent.

Resistance

Many students will, in the first instance, resist attempts to involve them in assessment of themselves because they lack confidence in their own powers, and feel that they are not capable of making important judgements about their own work. However, where students are asked to fill in a self-evaluative sheet on a piece of written work, for example, and are asked to assign to themselves a grade for what they have achieved, very often their outcomes are very similar to those of a third party, particularly where the criteria have been negotiated and are explicit at the outset.

Another form of resistance to self- and peer assessment is by students who feel, for example, that they have paid a great deal for the teaching that they are undertaking and that it is the job of the tutor to undertake this. At the University of Northumbria, for example, a group of MA legal practice students balked at the idea of having to undertake peer assessment because they felt that was the tutor's job that they had paid £4,500 to experience.

Resistance may also be experienced from a third agency, that is, from validation and review bodies who will need to be convinced of the validity and reliability of the system, without taking into account how commonly invalid and unreliable tutor assessment itself can be.

Although some students will resist the idea of self-assessment, a study at the University of Edinburgh reported that students in the history department and in the faculty of divinity responded positively to the idea that it should be a substantial part of degree assessment, although they felt that opportunities to undertake it at the moment were fairly limited (McRae, 1993). In the history department, 83 per cent felt that self-assessment should be developed a great deal or to some extent in formal courses, whereas it was only developed in some 32 per cent of courses. The same students, now in work, currently use self-assessment a great deal or to some extent, in 58 per cent of their cases.

Eighty-eight per cent of the divinity students felt that self-assessment should be developed in formal courses; 37 per cent said it had been developed in their courses, and 57 per cent said they were expected to use self-assessment in their working lives. Self-assessment, then, is a competence that is undeveloped within many degree courses but it is an essential working methodology required upon graduation.

It is students who do *not* know that they are competent and students who do not know that they are not yet competent, who have problems with their learning. In this way the development of self-evaluative skills is very powerful in improving students' own learning ability. Thus where students develop an awareness of their own abilities they are able effectively to research their own learning processes alongside the actual learning; this makes for more competent learning.

Self-assessment, on this analysis, is fundamental to learning, which is the business of HE. Boud (1990) developed this by arguing that 'traditional' assessment practices neither matched the world of work, nor encouraged effective learning. Summative goals dominated assessment, he said, often leading students to concentrate on a narrow range of skills and content, encouraging cue-seeking behaviour (trying to read the lecturer's mind), and leading students to focus on grades, not upon their achievements and areas in need of development. As we have seen, in summative assessment reliability takes precedence over validity. Furthermore, the students' ways of working were seldom assessed. It disempowered students and could act to demotivate them. He looked at the work of research students, showing how their job of writing a paper for publication differed radically from the behaviours which traditional assessments fostered. Self-assessment, he argued, is fundamental to all aspects of learning. Learning is an active endeavour and thus it is only the learner who can learn and implement decisions about his or her own learning: all other forms of assessment are therefore subordinate to it (Boud, 1990, p.109).

At its heart is the goal of promoting the reflective student, one who has a degree of self-directing independence and who is, therefore, well placed to be a lifelong learner. This is perhaps the main reason for valuing self-assessment, as a way of developing reflective individuals. Not only may self-assessment develop autonomy, it also opens up areas of learning, such as experiential learning, which are fundamentally inaccessible to tutors, which is one facet of its power for extending assessment, validly, to the process of learning. It needs to be appreciated, then, that self-assessment, in its fullest sense, means more than simply getting the learner to assess the match between criteria and performance. It also means negotiating and establishing appropriate criteria in the first place, as Stephenson and Weil (1992) show in their studies of Education for Capability. It also locates self-assessment more firmly at the formative end of the spectrum, for although it may be used summatively, the idea of negotiating criteria sits well with the notion of formative assessment and the development of a consciousness about one's own performance – a sort of metacognition (Sadler, 1989).

Quite simply, self-assessment fosters a different, more powerful view of the student than does traditional assessment. It also allows a wider range of students' learning to be documented, and in particular it provides a way for students' ways of working and thinking to be documented, perhaps through students keeping a reflective 'research diary'. On educational grounds, self-assessment is necessary where HE is seen as a way of developing knowledgeable, self-directing, reflective people. Its purposes may be summative, as we have said, but it is obvious that unless students have some self-critical awareness, of the sort which self-assessment promotes, then it is hard to see how they can benefit from formative assessment. Self-assessment, self-knowledge and formative assessment intertwine.

Accuracy and self-assessment

Researchers have tried to see how accurately students' self-assessments match those of their tutors. Good reviews of the literature are by Boud and Falchikov (1989) and Falchikov and Boud (1989). Some studies find that students tend to give themselves lower marks than their tutors (Mahalski, 1992), others that they give higher marks. Falchikov and Boud reported that in a meta-analysis of 57 qualitative studies, they found that on average students graded themselves higher than did 68 per cent of tutors marking their work. In a review of quantitative research they noted a slight tendency for older studies to report overrating and for more recent ones to report underrating. Moreover, high achievers were prone to underrate themselves, where low achievers tended to do the opposite (Boud and Falchikov,

1989). There are also some indications that first- and final-year students may be the most accurate at grading their own work and that self-assessments are more accurate in natural sciences than they are in social sciences. The safest conclusion seems to be that there is no consistent pattern of over- or under-estimation of one's own work compared to tutors' assessments. Nor does research show any pattern associated with the gender of learners.

Part of the skill of enabling students to assess themselves comes from enabling them to work out fairly accurately what they are good at and what they are not good at. There may be quite a lot of work that has to be done to get them to have a clearer and fairer assessment of their own competence. In some cases it will not be possible to convince overconfident students that they are not as good as they suggest, or perhaps to convince people with extremely low self-esteem that they are successful and competent in their learning.

There are no easy solutions to this problem, but the strategies to be used to combat it are the same as those that apply elsewhere in the assessment process, that is, the requirement to provide clear criteria for success or failure, and the justification of achievement with evidence. Students asked to prove their success in achieving a particular standard will not be able to do so if evidence is not forthcoming and students, in preparing evidence for a claim, may often be gratified by the success of what they have achieved.

It is important to remember that we can question the assumption that tutors accurately graded the student in the first place. The more an assignment demands the exercise of what Eisner (1985) called 'connoisseurship' – judgement, insight, originality, appreciation – the less likely there is to be agreement upon its quality. The more an assignment is closed, as in a natural science multiple-choice test, the easier it is to get agreement amongst graders, especially when compared to open-ended assignments of the sort that ask for the exercise of judgement in problematic and contested areas. In other words, we are making an unreliable comparison in asking how far student self-assessments agree with tutors' – it's far from obvious that tutor assessments are necessarily reliable.

Faculty assessments – ones done by tutors – are more reliable when the task is a closed one. Closed tasks – and many assignments in the natural sciences look closed – may readily be reliably assessed. Where a task is open, it can be 'tightened up' by agreeing, disseminating and sharing the criteria that will be used to evaluate performance. We have already noticed the claim that where assessments are criteria-referenced, then reliability is a question about the degree to which the performance properly meets the criteria. Some have gone so far as to say that therefore reliability entirely ceases to be an issue and that validity alone matters. Open tasks can be made more 'closed', without sacrificing their essential nature, by sharing the criteria by which they are to be judged.

Now, this not only offers a way of bringing tutor assessments more closely into line with each other (important though that is), but it also shows how self- and tutor assessments may be brought into greater harmony. Mahalski

(1992) showed that her 28 geography students (who were writing an essentially descriptive assignment, which was arguably closer to the closed than to the open end of the spectrum), tended to underestimate their grades because they used a different, wider range of criteria than did their assessors. Agreement on the criteria and on their meanings would have brought tutors and students closer together in their assessments.

Self-assessment and time-saving

The need to teach students to assess themselves means that the time saving to tutors may not be as great as is sometimes imagined. However, a departmental assessment programme that includes a number of measures, each of which produces only a small time-saving, may have quite a marked cumulative effect. Some forms of self-assessment do save time. Swanson *et al.* (1991) have shown how multiple-choice items can be used in the assessment of medical students' ability to resolve problems. Plainly, these are things that may be put on a self-assessment basis, possibly through the use of computer-based assessments, which would indicate to students the areas on which they should concentrate further. Gentle (1992) has described a computer-based system developed at Nottingham Trent University to support project work. Called THESYS, the programme is an expert system that is used by tutors in grading students' projects, and which students can use for formative and diagnostic purposes as they write their reports. In this way students assess their work and get a quality of insight that would hardly be available through other methods.

Approaches to self-assessment

The methods of self-assessment can be as varied as the imagination allows. One form that is often commended is the portfolio, which is discussed in more detail below. Records of Achievement are a closely related demonstration of achievement. Boud (1992) described a self-assessment regime in which students set goals, specify the criteria that define whether those goals have been met, describe the evidence that would be presented, set out a case for claiming that the goals have been met, wholly or in part, and lastly point to action that should follow from their evaluation. Students are positive about this, since they see it as fundamental to their learning. However, this is plainly more time-consuming than traditional practices, and students do complain that they lack the time for reflection.

Self-assessment forms can have all-round value. For example, they can give students an opportunity to evaluate their own performance in advance of submission by asking them to comment on what they feel they have achieved, how successful the piece of work is, what particular problems have been encountered, what the students would have to do in order to improve the grade that is being awarded, what aspects they feel unconfident about and what aspects they feel very confident about. Filling in these details will require students to put time and energy into evaluating their own performance. Where the tutor is in broad agreement with the student, a great deal of time can be saved for the tutor, and only when there is very great disagreement will a significant amount of tutor-written feedback need to be given in order to fill in the gaps and iron out any problems. Such an evaluation form will need to be supplemented either by extremely detailed self-assessment criteria or by model answers which enable students to see in relevant disciplines exactly what they are trying to achieve. We believe there is no better way to help students to understand exactly what is needed by them to achieve than to let them see anonymous good – and poor – work done by other students. A very successful exercise at the University of Northumbria at Newcastle has been to save work from a preceding year and let students look at a good, poor and average answer to a question that has been set in a previous year. This enables them to see exactly what they are trying to achieve, and by evaluating others' work they are better able to evaluate their own work.

To summarize: many assessment methods will be described in this section. We contend that it is not only the methods that are significant but also *who* assesses learners' work. We believe that learners should learn to assess their own learning. In the process, there may be some time-savings for academic staff, but the case is not based on parsimony so much as on the educational importance of becoming critical.

We note, but will not explore, the claim that self-assessment can be seen in a sinister light, interpreted as a way of making students discipline themselves to conform with values that are effectively imposed upon them.

Peer assessment

The relationship between self- and peer assessment

There are different schools of thought about where self- and peer assessment fit in together. Our belief is that the more sophisticated skill necessary is that of assessing oneself accurately, validly and reliably. We therefore propose, first, that students, using criteria provided by the tutor, should undertake peer assessment of other students. So, students watching a presentation by another individual or group of students, once they have in their hands a set of criteria to enable evaluation to take place, are, we feel, as competent at evaluating achievement of performance as almost anyone else.

Having got some skill at the assessment of people in other groups, then learners may try assessing peers within their own group, for example, when they have undertaken a group project to which all students have contributed. Having worked through inter-peer and intra-peer assessment, they will then have the skills necessary to evaluate better their own performances. Hence peer and self-assessment reinforce each other.

Self- and peer assessment: preparation

These methods provide no panacea for the problem of coping with increasing student numbers. It is mistaken to think that as workloads increase, the way to solve the tutors' problem with increased marking workload is simply to dump the work onto the students. It is possible that self- and peer assessment can to some extent save time, but this is by no means a simple equation because the energy and effort involved in self- and peer assessment tend to be 'front-loaded'. Learners need a great deal of preparation in order to help them achieve these processes. There has to be a great deal of time put into explaining, developing and negotiating the criteria which are to be used for assessment – which is the recurrent theme of this section on assessment methods.

Rehearsing peer assessment: the egg game

Students will need opportunities for rehearsal in a non-threatening situation in order that they can make mistakes and find out about the problems in a non-mark-carrying environment. For this reason, at the University of Northumbria we tend to run a briefing session at the beginning of an assignment that includes peer assessment, with an exercise that is relatively good fun, so that students can have a chance to find out the issues that are inherent in the process. If they are asked, for example, in small groups, to make a container to carry an egg which can be dropped from a height without breaking (the egg game), this can provide an opportunity for them to learn about peer assessment in an area completely unrelated to their own work. It has to be done very carefully so that the concentration is on process rather than product. We like to issue the materials and the eggs to groups of about five or six and then ask them to wait before they start the task until they have prepared the criteria on which they are to be assessed.

Once criteria have been established, the next thing that has to be determined is how much weighting is to be allocated to each mark; so, out of a mark of 20 how many marks each criterion will carry. Once the criteria and weighting have been agreed, it then remains to be decided whether what they are assessing is process or product and, this having been sorted out, they are then in a position to decide who will do the assessing: the tutor, the individual (self), peers in their own group (intra), or peers in the others' group (inter). Once all these stages have been undertaken the students are ready to begin the task and to complete the container. As this is going on, the tutor maintains a running-issues flipchart, which is discussed at the end of the process, once the egg-carrying mechanisms have been tried out and great hilarity has ensued.

This process enables students to think about what is involved in peer assessment and, at the same time, to raise any problems on issues such as collusion, fairness and validity that may arise.

Having undertaken a light-hearted task, they are then in a position to go ahead with the actual peer assessment which will then be part of the formal assessment process.

Another useful way of developing the skills of self- and peer assessment is to involve students in giving feedback, rather than in actually assessing each other at an early stage. For example, a group of students, at pre-submission stage, can look at each other's work, bearing in mind the criteria that had been negotiated in advance, and can therefore assess each other's work in an informal setting, giving feedback on strengths and weaknesses, prior to the submission of the piece of work. At the University of Northumbria at Newcastle this has been done with students on a communications course who were submitting CVs and letters of application for assessment. In groups of about five or six they reviewed each other's draft letters and CVs, and marked up errors and added comments. The role of the tutor was then much more that of a moderator who would either agree with the comments or disagree, giving positive feedback to the submitting student. In this way, a great deal of time for the tutor can be saved in weeding out minor errors, and the energies of the tutor can be concentrated on the macro issues.

Some problems

When people assess each other problems can arise, including the settling of old scores by giving other students bad marks. This can work the other way and students can, on occasions, over-mark each other's achievements because of friendship or loyalty. It is not surprising that a cohort students who have worked together all year will be unwilling to mark each other down, especially when the assessment counts towards end of unit assessment or indeed towards final degree classification. It is sometimes the case that students will collude to give each other high marks on the lines of 'we will give you a good mark, if you give us a good mark', and this also must be prevented.

In peer assessment students can sometimes be rather unsophisticated in their judgements and will on occasion give higher marks to the noisy, showy, extrovert members of the group and lower marks to the quieter members, who may equally have made significant contributions to the group process, but who tend not to make so much noise about it.

A fourth problem is the way in which sometimes idle or lazy students will ride on the backs of other students and thereby claim credit for work they haven't achieved. The converse of this is students who, for personal reasons, are unable to contribute fully and are carried by the group. This is not unlike the practice in employment where a member of a working group may well be underperforming because of divorce, family problems or personal illness, and other members of the group will carry this person for a limited period of time until patience, energy or capability runs out.

In order to ensure that peer assessment is valid it will be necessary to use systems to ensure that in each case *evidence* and *criteria* are taken into account.

If students are to be involved in assessing each other's posters, for example, there are dangers of collusion ('we'll mark you high and you mark us high') or retribution ('hey, they only gave us a four, we'll give them even less!'). At the University of Northumbria at Newcastle tutors have used a system where each group is numbered and the odds assess the evens and vice versa. Thus groups 1,3,5,7,9,11,13 and 15 could be asked to assess the even groups between 12 and 1 pm and groups 2,4,6,8,10,12,14 and 16 could assess the odds between 1 and 2 pm (it is equally possible to do it simultaneously but at two different venues). Using a peer assessment sheet that has been negotiated (or at least issued) at the briefing session, the groups can then review and grade half of the posters produced by their cohort. The assessment sheet can be very simple or much more complex, whatever is 'fit for the purpose'. We have found that significant learning is taking place at the time when students as a group are analysing each other's work. Discussion of how far another group has achieved a programme brief, how innovative is the solution, how viable is the suggested outcome, how effectively it has been portrayed and how visually effective a poster is, will tend to hone the assessing students' critical faculties and enable them to perform better themselves on a subsequent poster exercise. Assessment becomes a genuine learning experience.

Who marks?

The problems of peer assessment are similar to those of self-assessment, basically amounting to an unease that the assessment is not done by the 'expert', that is, by the tutor. The response to this worry is also similar. There are some things that tutors can judge better than can students, but they are not as numerous as might be assumed. It might be thought that only a history tutor could judge whether an essay on Charles I showed a good knowledge of the sources and of the secondary literature, drawing them together to form a persuasive case. However, that cannot be true: surely anyone who had studied the same field could assess those points? Furthermore, where criteria have been established, the expert has made his or her expertise available to students, giving them guidance on the key features of skilled – and less skilled – performances. So, not only could students assess each other but also there would be considerable benefit in doing so, since in assessing each other they would be applying, purposefully, criteria of worth that they need to develop in their own work. Through using these criteria they could be learning them. Through peer assessment students would be learning, which is, as we repeatedly argue, the main purpose of assessment. Writing of mechanical engineering, Forbes and Spence (1992) described a system where students would complete some 50–60 'standard' problems that they would mark in class. Through the marking, students became more familiar with the best way of presenting their solutions, while the format of students marking each other's work in class proved to be an efficient way of marking large amounts of work (there were 170 students in the group).

Likewise, King *et al.* (1992) had mechanical engineering students mark each other's reports, each of about 1,000 words. A more open-ended activity than marking standard problems, this entailed two students marking each report and staff monitoring their marking. Analysis of the results led the authors to conclude that 'marker variability was not regarded as being of serious concern' (p.24). Most (70 per cent) of the students felt that this helped them with their report writing, while half also believed they had a better grasp of the subject matter thanks to this peer marking. However, Verran *et al.* (1993), writing of groupwork in applied biological sciences, rehearsed the familiar problems of students over-rewarding each other and the difficulty which staff had in trying to monitor individuals' contributions to the work. They found that these problems were eased by requiring students to keep a log of their activities; by making criteria much tighter and more explicit; and by introducing a procedure for discriminating amongst the several members of a group, so that staff could then apply a multiplier to the group mark in order to reward individuals' contributions fairly.

As with self-assessment there can be checks, if they are needed, with tutors also participating and students having the right to have a tutor's assessment; yet this may be no more necessary than with self-assessment. Race (1992) has claimed that his judgements of students' oral presentations tally with peer assessments, and the same has been said of first-year pharmacology presentations at Leeds University. At the University of Northumbria at Newcastle it has been remarkable how closely averaged peer marks have matched tutor marks for poster displays. This is perhaps unsurprising when the nature and level of briefing on criteria are taken into account. On occasions it has felt as if the tutor's role has become almost superfluous, although students still like to have the tutor taking part in the process, often because they are proud of their achievements and want to show them off.

One danger arises in the sheer mathematics of multiple assessors. If 20 or so groups assess each other and two categories of staff are also involved, and there is an element of oral assessment too (eg, 'How effective were the group in answering questions on the poster?'), then the processing of all the assessment sheets can be a nightmare. For this reason we advise simplicity, certainly in the first attempt, and the use of students themselves, under supervision, to undertake the averaging of peer assessment marks.

Peer assessment is seen as related to self-assessment, both as a way of strengthening learners' skill at self-assessment and as a complement to self-assessment. Given the importance which employers of all sorts put upon the ability to work as a part of a team, it is important that learners in HE are exposed to situations which require them to respond sensitively and perceptively to peers' work. As in employment, those who we judge now are ones with whom we shall be working again. Much can be learned about leading teams and working within a team through the experience of peer assessment.

Assessing groups

Tutors may feel the need to assess groups if they are worried that individuals in groups may be treated unfairly, either through their contributions being overlooked in favour of more extrovert or more pushy colleagues, or by students claiming to have undertaken tasks which they have not actually achieved. There are a number of ways of coping with this particular problem.

The first is the simplest and no worse for that. The group mark for an assignment which has been completed by a number of students will be identical for all the students. If this is the case it should not carry a large proportion of marks; it should be lightly weighted. If all students get the same marks, there will be some inequality creeping in but this is the most simple methodology for coping with assessing student groups.

Second, the product – whether it is a lab report, a poster display, a piece of writing, or a presentation – will be assessed and awarded a mark. If students have been awarded 17 out of 20 and there are 6 students, this gives a total of 102 marks available. Students can then themselves, by negotiation relying on criteria and evidence, allocate within their own group a mark per person which must not exceed 20 out of 20 and can be as low as the students feel appropriate, so that the aggregate mark achieved equals 102. For example, a student who did very little could be awarded 10 or 12 out of 20, and a student who had carried the group and had done a great deal would be allocated 20 marks, so long as the total did not exceed 6 x 17. This allows a great deal of flexibility and enables credit to be given where credit is due, but on occasions we have experienced students colluding together to all give each other the same mark. In some ways, if they do this it is difficult to perceive what the problem is, because if they are all happy about it, then it seems a reasonably fair process. Sally Brown has on occasions used this methodology and suggested that she would viva any student groups where the peer assessment seemed problematic or exciting to her. This has worked extremely well.

Another method that has been seen to work is that all students would get the same mark, say 17 out of 20, for the product, but they would, in addition, get another set of marks, maybe a mark out of 10, awarded by the peers within the group for their individual contribution in terms of teamwork, initiation of ideas and contribution to the general running of the project.

A further method is to break down the group task into clearly identified tasks and when the product is assessed each student's individual contribution would be attributed and assessed separately. The problem with this lies in the fact that when sharing out group tasks it is not always easy to do so fairly. Some students could argue reasonably that the task they were allocated was much more difficult than somebody else's, so it is not surprising that they didn't manage as much, and other students may say that the task they were awarded was very easy and they therefore did not have a particular chance to shine. However, on some occasions, this method might be useful.

One more possibility is that students be awarded the same mark, say 17 out of 20, for the product but that there should be, at the end of the unit or semester, an opportunity for students in final examinations to answer an exam question which is based on the group project, but which requires the student to build on the experiences and knowledge achieved in this exercise and to answer an exam question accordingly. That is not to say that they will be double-tested; what it means is, for example, if students have been looking at an engineering design problem, that particular design problem might form the starting point for a test of skill at calculation, or for a case study which they will be asked to write about during an examination question.

Broadening the range

Much traditional assessment has been of work in written form: exam scripts, essays, reports, dissertations, theses and so on. Some disciplines have also incorporated assessments in a wider range of media. In language teaching, for example, oral work has normally been part of the process, and in medicine, students expect to have vivas as well as written exams. Disciplines such as theatre studies would be meaningless without assessments of live performance, and in fine art and fashion on-the-spot critiques are an essential part of the learning process. Live projects and case studies form an integral part of many subjects' assessment processes.

Assessment can involve a wide range of media beyond the word on the page. Audio tapes, video tapes, photographs, sketches, diagrams, paintings, posters, maps, charts, graphs, computer discs and printouts have all been employed as ways in which the student can record and demonstrate achievement.

Some factors apply across a wide range of assessment methods. We may wish, for example, to set a cash limit on a particular assignment so that students who cannot afford extensive photocopying and photography, who do not have access to family camcorders and word-processors, who have no free supply of raw materials for models and exhibition material, should not be disadvantaged. In the past, typed work was the exception; increasingly now it is the norm and indeed we tend to expect fairly high standards of desk-top publishing for important pieces of work. We must keep in mind that students are at the same time becoming progressively more impoverished.

We need also to consider how a varied assessment pattern might affect students' stress levels. Just as in schools, where perceived stress levels increased with the move towards continuous assessment through what seemed to the candidates to be unending and continual assignments, so also we can expect that students faced with a range of different kinds of assignments may well feel overwhelmed. However, this should be set against the fact that traditional examinations have also provided heavy stress levels for some candidates – exams, after all, are best at testing which students are best at passing exams!

We advocate, then, that assessment is best when varied, both in methods of assessment and in media of response, because every method disadvantages *some* students, so the fairest way is to provide a variety of methods.

Other considerations in assessing fairly

Great care must be taken to minimize systematic, albeit subliminal, bias in grading. There is a whole range of difficulties that can creep in.

In the first instance, it is very possible to allow personal preference, likes and dislikes of particular students, to affect one's judgement when marking students' work. Many tutors will recognize the syndrome whereby, on picking up a particular student's work, their heart either lifts or their soul groans because they have expectations about what they will find. A lot of problems can creep in when students and tutors are very friendly, particularly when they are having relationships. One of the reasons why universities are currently looking at banning consensual sexual relationships between tutors and students is that they fear that personal bias and prejudice may creep in to assessment schedules.

Certainly, there seems to be evidence that gender and race can affect the grades that students get. For example, there is evidence suggesting that female students tend to underperform in relation to male students. In particular, the proportion of firsts awarded to female students tends to be lower than that for male students *unless anonymous marking is used*. Where anonymous marking is used, this difference disappears almost entirely and this must give us an indication of some of the problems that exist around gender and marking.

Similarly, there has been much concern recently about the fact that in Law Society finals resits, black students have a much lower chance of succeeding than white students. One of the reasons for this is that the assessment here is not written assessment but assessment of a student's interpersonal and communication skills, as recorded on video. Most tutors will recognize the value of anonymous written assignment because they can see that this is relatively easy to do. What is much more difficult is anonymously to mark oral presentations, role-plays and group activities in order to reduce race and gender bias.

There are, however, strategies that can be utilized in order to prevent this, the most obvious being that there must be a heavy reliance on evidence that overt criteria have been met. However, the other safeguard against prejudice, however unconscious it may be, is to use triangulation in some form or another, so that the assessment is not relying purely on one person's, possibly subjective, response. This could be, for example, using double-marking, tutor sample marking of each other's work, peer assessment and self-assessment. In any case, it is always valuable to make sure that whenever gender and race are apparent in students' work, it is taken as read that there should be cross-checking to ensure that prejudice does not creep into the process. The strategies can also be safeguards against the effects of tutors' personal likes and dislikes.

Chapter 6:

Assessment on the Page

Essays

Essays are commonplace and often tiresome to mark, so that assessors are in danger of ending up like Mr Krook in Bleak House: he disappeared in a puff of smoke caused by spontaneous self-combustion. If assessors do not become clearer about why they set essays, the equivalent fate, academically speaking, looms.

If we critically inspect what really needs to be assessed in our subject, this might be only a portion of what would be demonstrated in a full, completed essay. We need to ask why, then, we should have to mark a full essay if much of what it reveals is superfluous to our present assessment needs? (Andresen *et al.*, 1993, p.17).

Essays tend to be ballasted with information and copious references to stock sources. Marks are largely awarded for what the learner makes of that knowledge, yet this is definitely the minor part of the essay. Indeed, in most essays, the urge to convince the assessor that the learner knows something about the main areas of information is disastrous. The introduction tells us what blocks of knowledge are to be covered but not how they will lead to a certain conclusion, let alone revealing that there are substantial conceptual ambiguities in the title anyway. The blocks follow one another like coal wagons on a train, although the links between the blocks are less obvious, amounting only to the fact that one follows another in some arbitrary way, until the tail-light of the conclusion is reached. This glimmer is often marked by an announcement that 'it has now been proved that . . .', at which point it disappears from sight.

In his work on essay writing at Lancaster, Hounsell (1984) distinguished between essays that were collections or arrangements (and which gained modest marks) and those which were presented as arguments, gaining the top marks. He had an intermediate category of 'viewpoint' essays where students tended to ignore inconvenient facts, presenting personalized interpretations rather than sustained and comprehensive arguments in which there was an on-going interplay of data and interpretations. Interestingly, he found that students' marks were more influenced by their conceptions of essay writing (argument, viewpoint or arrangement) than by their planning methods. Different approaches to planning were associated with each of the conceptions of essay writing and it was the conceptions which correlated with the grades awarded, not the planning processes. The conclusion is that in arts subjects at least, helping students to do better involves helping them to understand what an 'argument' essay comprises. We think that typical, rather unreflective essay practices, containing the assumption that students 'really' know how to write essays, are being supported by endemic assessment practices. We suggest that it is better to interweave the assessment and learning processes so that students get plentiful practice at writing introductions, making link paragraphs (which summarize the argument to date and presage the course it is about to take) and devising interesting conclusions.

Learners might understand this better if mark schemes were more widely used, always assuming that the schemes valued argument rather than arrangement. There is a case for saying that in arts subjects this would amount to pre-specifying responses which by their very nature should not be pre-specified. Yet this cannot be the same as saying that it is not possible to identify the characteristics of a good account of, say, the reasons why Blake's 'Proverbs of Hell' is best understood as the core of *Songs of Innocence*. It does mean that the actual answer is open, not that its characteristics are ineffable. As ever, clarifying and negotiating criteria matter.

Our last suggestion is to set more part-essays, constrained-format essays and 'modified essay questions'. Excellent models of essay style are the leader articles in the quality press and book reviews in the better academic journals. Setting more constrained items of this sort is not popular, since learners do find them hard. And they are hard because it forces them away from the habit of filling up space with information, towards a recognition that information is useful, like Krook's currency, in proportion to the degree that it is used. The related strategy of requiring part-essays does much the same. Students might be asked to write a 300-word introduction; note headings amounting to 500 words to indicate the main content to be covered; two link paragraphs amounting to 100 words each to be located at sensible points in the previous section; and a 500-word conclusion. That, we insist, is usually more demanding than setting a 5,000-word item. And easier to mark. And, usually, much more interesting to mark.

A colleague at Lancaster has recently secured faculty approval to replace 7,000 words of coursework, weighted at 50 per cent of the unit, with two 1,000-word essays weighted at 40 per cent of the unit. These items are to be critical commentaries in response to novel photocopied material given to the students. To review it adequately they have to draw upon the range of insights gained in the course, doing things such as:

- discussing the typicality of the ideas in the extracts
- analysing and commenting on the key elements
- identifying stated and unstated assumptions
- elaborating intended and unintended consequences
- considering criticisms
- commenting on distinctiveness
- assessing the relevance and cogency of the criticisms
- offering a personal and argued interpretation.

Cogency, he noted, will be a criterion applied to determine the grade awarded.

Exams and time-constrained, individual assessment

Examinations are often said to be a very efficient form of assessment because all students sit the exam at the same time, and a pile of scripts can be relatively easily marked, especially if marking is only summative and not formative.

Schoolteachers have got the irritating habit of referring to SATs (these are examination-like Standard Assessment Tests) as 'assessment', as if everything else were really frippery. So too with universities, where examinations are often seen as the 'real' form of assessment, the reliable 'gold standard'.

Examinations do have value but, as with all assessment techniques, some thought is needed if the best results are to be had. In particular, it is important to scrutinize the common practice of allowing students extensive choice within an examination paper, which can mean that no two students effectively sit the same examination. The examination becomes invalid, and students are not required to show mastery of the course as a whole. Besides, three- or four-question papers do not lead to high reliability. Examinations based on a good number of shorter questions would lead to greater reliability. Many examinations make considerable demands on learners' factual knowledge, which can have the unfortunate side-effect of encouraging cramming and shallow learning at the expense of that 'deep' learning which is HE's avowed goal.

Truly, many examinations encourage surface learning, but it has to be said that they also can allow the student who has gained a deeper understanding of the subject throughout the course to show it. Moreover, there is no reason why all examinations should share features which are now common and which encourage 'cramming' behaviour. Students might be given the option of taking examinations under a proffered degree scheme. This is a scheme under which a degree classification is proffered to the student on the basis of coursework. The student has the option of trying to improve this classification by taking examinations which can only improve on it. It would be particularly important, though, that the coursework had been well thought through to match programme aims.

Even summative examinations, though, can have considerable power to encourage learning, partly through providing that extrinsic motivation which is so necessary (though we're not denying the importance of intrinsic motivation). They also provide a point at which the best learners review all of their work and look for – perhaps even find – patterns which were not to be seen earlier. Examinations can provide a stimulus for understanding to be developed through deep learning. The fact that this is often not the case is disappointing, and it is worth wondering what might be done to get learners to treat examinations as a force for the formation of new, better understandings. When setting examinations, it is advisable that tutors should think about what students should actually be doing during that time. Is it necessary that they should actually be writing at length for the whole period, or is it possible that some elements of the examination could take the form of summaries or reviews, which might be much shorter in length, representing just as much student thinking and workload but not so much text?

There is nothing new about different examination formats, especially ones like open-book examinations, seen papers and take-away examinations. Variations on these themes exist, so that a learner taking an oral examination in German might have prepared three agreed topics, one of which would be chosen at random to be the subject of the viva.

In essence, though, open-book examinations allow students access to materials during a traditional examination, so that it is not dominated by the panic of trying to remember formulae, dates or declensions. Peter Knight remembers doing an open-book Latin examination in which most of the tricky phrases (and he found most of the phrases tricky) were translated in the dictionary as examples of how the key word was used in classical times. It became a case of stringing together the dictionary translations, keeping an eye on the grammar and the best way of making nice sense of the resulting patchwork. Cheating? Well, as a professional historian, this is how he would have worked in the library, and it could be said that the result was a perfectly valid test of Knight's skill as a medieval historian (which rather alarmingly proved to be better than his skill at anything else).

In-tray exercise

We have noted and admired an innovative form of examination which attempts to assess working competences more effectively than a formal three-hour written exam. At the start of a day-long exam, candidates for accountancy examinations, for example, are given a dossier or in-tray of papers to read through. This models in some ways the real-life working practice of accountants who have to wade through piles of papers, not all of which may be relevant. The skills lie in seeing what is and is not important.

Later in the day, candidates are set a task, such as producing a balance sheet, that relies on their effectiveness at sifting data. As the exam progresses, variant information and tasks can be introduced, so that by the end of the exam, students have realistically simulated working in the accountancy context. We would argue that this kind of exam more effectively tests appropriate skills and knowledge than traditional essay-type questions could ever do.

Seen papers are similarly based on the principle that people do not normally have to solve unexpected problems in 45 minutes. This section of our book is a collaborative effort, worked and reworked, thought and rethought. So, should not learners be treated likewise, given time to prepare their examination answers? This is not uncommon in arts and social science subjects, perhaps because the diversity of possible answers to any particular question means that the scope for collaboration that amounts to cheating is curbed. An examination paper on Dickens' later novels might be released a week in advance, allowing students time to re-read these far-from-slim books, perhaps re-appreciating them, thereby learning through assessment. Talk and collaboration would invariably take place, which is surely all to the good, since what matters is not so much where learners get ideas but how sharp they are at realizing which ideas could be used, how ideas might be linked to or contrasted with other ideas, and how sensitive they are to bringing it all together in a pithy answer.

Disadvantages are that students might exploit the system by idling throughout the course, gambling all on inspired preparation for 'seen' examinations. Another possible problem is plagiarism, an obsessive worry in some universities. A rogue male might get a talented colleague to prepare an answer for him. The best way of countering this also takes away some of the attraction of take-away examinations. Examinees might be given the topic of examination but not the exact question, so that the examination remained an assessment of the individual. Alternatively, they might be given just a morning's notice of the questions (as happens with Lancaster history special subject papers). Where the examination is oral, a learner's excessive reliance on others can become apparent. We should remember, though, that take-away examinations can work against students who have caring responsibilities which limit the time they have for this form of examination preparation.

An interesting application of the seen examination paper was devised by a psychology department. At the *beginning* of the course the (substantial) examination paper was issued to students. The complaint that this was 'cheating' was met with the reply that when students could answer all the questions on this (substantial) paper, they would have mastered the course. This is a bold example of an assessment-led curriculum.

If we identify the key elements of examinations, we can see rather better how they might be developed in harmony with programme aims and, of course, that means that there will remain a place for the traditional three-hour essay paper, which is an excellent test of many features of many courses:

- exams are guaranteed to test the individual on his or her own: worries about plagiarism and excessively enthusiastic collaboration are banished from the exam room
- they are time-constrained, reflecting the need in life to work swiftly, under pressure and well
- they usually require students to draw together learning from many parts of the course.

Now, these characteristics may be maintained by many forms of 'examination'. Consider a system in which an accounting student prepares a computer program to cope with a defined situation, perhaps maintaining the accounts for a hotel. These are given to students and time is allocated for them to configure their spreadsheets, using software with which they are familiar. The examination involves them loading their programs under supervision and using them to tackle, in a set time, accounting problems relating to the hotel. Collaboration is not allowed. A student who does not fully understand the program or who has devised a clumsy or deficient spreadsheet will penalize him- or herself in the examination, which is in many ways a lifelike, valid and reliable test of the individual.

Or, again, where the 'examination' consists of the accumulated scores in several 15-minute class tests. A third example: a case study is prepared by tutors, who issue all students with a reader describing it some time before the examination. The examination consists of questions relating to the case study which require demonstrations of understanding of, say, the processes by which a marketing plan might be produced for the company in case. This form of open-book examination avoids one of the problems common to the type, which is that students promptly besiege the library to get books on the questions in the paper.

Examinations have a bad name amongst students, are viewed ambiguously by staff and are often derided by educationists. We have argued that if we hold on to the core features of examinations it is possible to produce a powerful set of techniques for time-constrained individual assessment.

Memoranda

Students often confuse quality with volume, with the result that written work can be voluminous in quantity but largely irrelevant or derivative. In many disciplines, the memorandum report can be of great value, requiring students to summarize findings on to a single page of A4 that might otherwise run to many pages. This kind of report can be used a in a wide variety of disciplines wherever some element of individual research is undertaken.

The advantages of using the A4 memorandum report are self-evident in that they are faster to mark than the typical lengthy report, but they stretch students' communication abilities. It is much more difficult to be succinct than it is to ramble, and the skill of summarizing is typically one that is widely required in science, industry and business. Such reports are less bulky to carry around than full-size ones and are easier and cheaper to photocopy, so students can retain their own copies and not risk loss (by tutor or student) of a single copy.

The students still have to undertake the same amount of research or practical work in order to complete the work, but do not have to copy out pages of repetitive methods or equipment lists that often bulk out the traditional lab report but which often form part of the briefing sheet in any case.

A sample memorandum form might look like this:

Memorandum report
Title:
(This should be a detailed and informative title which summarizes what might otherwise form an introduction.)
Author: Date:
Course: Receiving tutor:
Terms of reference:
(In this section, the student should summarize the background to the work, what was set out to be done, the parameters of the work and so on. This would normally be one or two paragraphs in length.)
Findings:
(This would form the bulk of the text and would take up most of the rest of the available space. Tutors may permit both sides of the A4 sheet to be used if required. Where appropriate, graphs, tables and figures can be provided as appendices.)
Results and conclusions:
(In this section students should summarize what they have achieved, what the implications of the work are and what further needs to be done. This section should not normally exceed a couple of paragraphs.)

Course readers

As an alternative to writing an essay on a topic, history students at Lancaster produce an edited collection of articles on a topic: a course reader. This involves them in evaluating and selecting material for inclusion. They also produce editorial commentary, which shows their grasp of the topic as a whole. The product is an intelligent and principled selection which, with its attendant introduction, is available for future generations of students to use in their studies.

The application of this technique is rather constrained by copyright and printing costs, yet it is an interesting technique, not least because it demands that learners try to synthesize the several parts of their course, selecting what seems to be crucial and illustrating controversies about that point in the most apposite way.

This is a group venture. The course reader is given a global mark (say 240) which the four students then divide amongst themselves, according to their various contributions.

Some colleagues use a variant of this where learners produce annotated reading lists on a topic. The tutor often provides a basic, un-annotated list, which the students both extend and evaluate, sharing their thoughts with their seminar group.

Dissertations and theses

These are traditional, being the classic method of examination of a candidate for a Master's degree in ancient universities. At their best they can be demanding, requiring the ability to handle large quantities of information, to analyse, criticize and evaluate it, to plan a programme of study designed to test the thesis, and then to present the whole in a coherent, compelling and pleasing form. Dissertations and theses (D and T) are book-writing in miniature, and as such they too can be very valid ways of assessing learners against certain course aims.

From being an élite assessment activity in the swamps of the Isis, they have become almost a requirement of every Bachelor of Arts programme. We suggest that this, in a mass system of HE, has intensified problems in assessment by D and T, perhaps with a greater risk of plagiarism or unfair practice. Dissertations are reports that are based upon readings that will often be unknown to the assessor and which, in the days of word-processors and optical scanners, may well be too freely incorporated into the learner's work. A solution is to set the learner a problem and a context in which to work. This would hardly tackle a more fundamental problem. Writing a good dissertation is hard, and partly a matter of luck. Professor Sir Geoffrey Elton has said that the only people who read PhD theses are examiners, who are paid for it, which points to the dullness and sterility of the exercise in so many cases. Part of the problem is that if one is to write ten 1,000-word reviews, the need to be incisive and impressive means that the learner's thought will need to be well to the fore. With a 10,000-word dissertation there will be sloughs of literature reviews, accounts of the context and descriptions of the methodology. Worse still, the writer will often conclude merely by pointing out that they've finished, leaving the reader unsure whether to be glad, or to wish that they continued and never submitted the thesis for assessment.

What we are arguing is that the form is in danger of triumphing over the content. Of course we should encourage investigations of the sort that launch dissertations, but require reports to be accompanied by executive summaries of no more than 1,000 words and which dwell upon the significance of the conclusions. A self-assessment sheet should also accompany the dissertation. The assessor would then concentrate on these documents, checking their grounding in the longer dissertation when appropriate. Vivas might become a common adjunct. Overall, we expect this to reduce the considerable time burdens of marking dissertations. We think that this approach is also well suited to projects and extended problem-working activities. This would make them much better tests of learners' abilities to learn and explain about their learning. As such they could be used formatively, but since they take a lot of time to do, they are likely to be given summative purposes.

There is scope for something longer than an essay but shorter than a dissertation, which students prepare in one term for presentation to other learners in the following term. This gives the work a purpose, capitalizes on the claim 'that to teach is to learn twice', provides the student with feedback, and could introduce an element of peer assessment.

Gobbets

A gobbet is a snippet of text, or picture or other brief stimulus presented to the student, who is then to respond to it. Typically this will involve identifying the stimulus, explaining its context and offering an opinion of its significance. Gobbets might include a picture of the joints in the iron bridge at Ironbridge Gorge, a nineteenth-century depiction of Columbus landing in America (sic), a Tom Keating painting, the title page of Wynken de Worde's (names do seem to be duller nowadays) *A Lyttell Geste of Robyn Hode*, or the opening sentence of Anthony Burgess' *Earthly Powers*.

Just as we were arguing that projects that are currently assessed by dissertations might better be dealt with by short, focused products, so gobbets are a sawn-off version of the essay. As such they promise greater assessment reliability, since students can do three gobbets, say, in the time that might be taken to write one essay. This may not be too welcome to students whose assessment strategy is to turn their right to choose examination questions (for example) to their advantage by concentrating on a slice of the course. We have already discussed how this can vitiate course aims (see also Andresen *et al.*, 1993). Gobbets and other short-answer items offer a solution.

They emerged in history special subject courses, where assessors were eager to be sure that students had actually read the set documents, rather than sloping off and just reading the secondary sources. For similar reasons they are to be found in English courses. Usually, then, they are associated with a corpus with which learners are expected to be familiar. They are quite good at this purpose, but we can see here the danger that the effect will be to encourage students to concentrate on learning to recognize and locate likely gobbets. The assessors' wish to invite evaluation, criticism and appreciation – to stimulate, in other words – can easily be lost. But perhaps this is the way of the world?

Journalism

It can be useful to augment traditional written assignments with articles for newspapers and magazines, either as an exercise or as a real submission. Students can be encouraged, for example, to write a short article on recent developments in surface coatings technology for an appropriate magazine, rather than writing a long essay or report on the subject. The advantage of such a task is that it requires an equivalent level of research, but will normally be shorter in length and probably easier to read and mark. On occasions students may be asked to write for different kinds of publication, so developing understanding of different audiences and contexts.

The skills of writing concisely and to the point in an accessible manner are valuable skills for any student in any discipline, and there is always the possibility that students can actually get work published, which may be useful for CVs and portfolios. The idea can be taken a stage further with a course or department magazine being produced to disseminate, for example, knowledge of each other's research projects, and the copy provided by individuals or small teams could provide the medium for an in-course assessment.

Projects

Most tutors will at some stage have faced a pile of written projects which are derivative, tedious, full of unreferenced, photocopied, unacknowledged material, which represent a vast amount of student work but do not represent a vast amount of student learning. When students are asked to undertake a project, it must be made clear at the outset that what they are not doing is putting together everything they can find on a subject. The crucial point is the briefing at which the specific outcomes of the activity are made clear either by tutors' direction or by negotiation.

So, instead of setting very broad project outlines which students then take away and work to undirected, we suggest that either very much tighter briefing is given or the assessment of project work is based on an incremental approach. In this way, students will be required to hand in staged elements of a project, so that renegotiation and direction can be given before energies are wasted in working to the wrong direction. In this way they can also be given credit for the process of producing a project – for systematic literature search, for time management and for organizational strategies. This may seem at first like increasing the assessment burden for the tutor, but by asking to see staged elements of work, the tutor then avoids the massive pile of project material landing on his or her desk at the submission date, all of which is completely unseen by the tutor. Where students have submitted elements in draft at stages, then the final assessment is made much simpler because at least the bulk of the material is, or should be, familiar to the tutor before the final assessment is made. This is particularly important where the project has a heavy assessment weighting; where the opportunities for disaster are great when students have little guidance throughout the preparation of the project.

Assessing active learning – problem-working and completion exercises

It is well known that problems do not exist in the wild. Situations do exist in which people may become uneasy and begin to feel that something ought to be done. Incrementally – silently – perhaps, someone or a group becomes the owner of that situation. They begin to conceive of a problem and they worry that problem into a shape and a form so that they can deal with it. They chafe away and produce recommendations or take action so that the situation becomes different. The unease may go away, but it's more likely that new concerns emerge, that the actions have consequences that someone will eventually see as problematic.

Take transport policy, for example. It is far from obvious that there is an area called 'transport' that can be thought about as an entity. Even if there is, it's not certain what ought to cause unease, let alone how unease might be resolved. What we do know is that 'solving' the problem of London's congestion by building the M25 didn't do much to 'solve' the 'problem' but it did create lots of new ones. Every solution is its own problem in an eternal dialectic.

The best test of such problem-working skill is through fieldwork, whether in a law firm, a school, hospital, social work attachment or engineering partnership. Typically, the learner will be told that during the course of the attachment a problem situation is to be identified, conceptualized and acted upon. The action is to be monitored and, through reflection, conclusions are to be drawn and further actions envisaged. However, mentors may be able to judge the actions, but universities also want some way of judging the reflection. A popular device is the reflective log/diary/journal. This is an account of the learner's engagement with the problem situation. It provides a description of what happened and what was done, which may be corroborated by the mentor. It should also be an account of the process of thought or reflection behind those actions: a public account of an internal dialogue. As such it should show the interplay between propositional and procedural thinking, between practice and the world of theory and generalization. Writing these journals is not easy and learners ought to be trained, perhaps through practising keeping journals relating to case studies or simulations studied at the university. They need to be clear about the audience for the journal and about its purpose.

A good alternative to reflective diaries lies in the critical incident technique. Learners identify a critical incident in a given period, explaining why they see it as a critical incident, analysing its characteristics, reflecting upon their actions and the choices which had been open to them, considering the outcomes and saying what they have learned from it.

Oral examinations are also a good way of examining students' problem-working abilities, always given that the subject of the examination is their own practice. Orals allow for follow-up questions and probing in a way denied to other forms of assessment.

Lastly, there is assessment through case studies which are presented at the university, with students being asked to identify what they regard as the most salient problem, to explain why, to suggest strategies for alleviating it, to explain how they might monitor the effect of their actions and suggest criteria by which they might judge the degree of success of their actions. Similar to case studies are simulations and games, which are case studies with action and feedback. These may well be computer-based.

Chapter 7:

Assessment off the Page

Aesthetics

Many degree courses incorporate the assessment of aesthetic elements; these courses include, for example, creative writing, fine art, sculpture, furniture design and landscape gardening. In each case, they obviously require the assessment of techniques, for example, techniques of painting, drawing, wood planing, stonemasonry and technical competence in language for use in writing poetry. But as well as these, there is an element that needs to be assessed that is based on how beautiful, how aesthetically pleasing the final outcome is, and problems always arise here in that these tend to be subjective decisions.

In the past, a great mystique has surrounded assessment for creative art, based largely on a master/apprenticeship relationship which indicates that the master has the power to decide whether the apprentice's achievement is aesthetically pleasing or not. This does not sit well with a competence-based approach to assessment in which the criteria for assessment are explicit and overt. Just as in assessment of business studies, history or engineering, it is often valuable to provide indications of what makes a first-class answer, a 2:1 answer, a 2:2 answer, a third answer and a fail; so, too, we would argue, it is very helpful for students being prepared for assessment of aesthetic products to be given guidance. Some would argue that this might stifle individuality and creativity, but we believe that such guidance would at least remove the current unfairness of many assessment systems of aesthetic products where the students are expected to guess what is in the mind of the assessor through the development of some kind of personal, mystical, aesthetic competence that has been kept hidden from the candidate.

One way round this is to accept that there is an element of subjectivity in assessment of aesthetic product, and, in our opinion, there is no harm in this so long as this is made plain. Obviously when a candidate is having a piece of writing assessed by a creative writing teacher, they would like to know how good the candidate is at writing lines that scan, using alliteration, assonance, figurative language and so forth. However, it isn't sufficient for the assessor simply to provide a grade and a number without giving feedback on these elements and also on those elements that are subjective. It is very likely that in aesthetic subjects criteria which are applied are partly the result of negotiation between the tutors and the learners.

It isn't just in the so-called 'creative arts', however, that this element of aesthetic judgement is made in assessment. For example, in assessing computer programs, very often an element of the marks is given for the elegance of the solution found; and in engineering there is sometimes an aesthetic element in the assessment of the shape of a ship's hull and so forth. Ultimately, we would say, it is the *recognition* of an element of subjectivity that is important. It isn't good enough for a fine art lecturer or the sculptor to say 'well, we know when we see a good sculpture or painting, and therefore we assess that as a first class one'. It is necessary for the students to be let in on the secret.

However, even in fine art or sculpture it is normally the case that there is a written component to the assessment and more traditional methods of assessment may, to some extent, provide a level of equivalence in marking there.

Creative productions

In some disciplines the medium of production will necessarily be in the form of a creative production of some kind. Students on the creative and performing arts degree at the University of Northumbria at Newcastle have, for example, taken part in activities such as productions of plays and musical performances. They have organized book fairs, exhibitions and play schemes for children involving creative activities. They have co-ordinated or organized community arts activities such as festivals or collective mural creation. They have worked as a whole team, as small groups and also been involved in individual solo performances in their own disciplines (music, painting, sculpture, dance, theatre studies, etc.).

Assessment of these kinds of activities is a complex process, requiring aesthetic as well as academic judgements to be made. The course team for such a programme needs to rely heavily on explicit and overt criteria in order that its judgements are valid and reliable. The tutors rely not just on their own professional judgements, based on their experiences as practitioners in the various fields, but also on a sound and well-debated set of agreed criteria for judging students' abilities against a set of standards which have to be flexible but objective.

Some aspects of these courses will be assessable through formal exams, but for the most part these will be inappropriate. More suitable would be the use of case studies, learning contracts, portfolios and the artefacts themselves.

Poster displays

Assessment in the teaching room is a very attractive option; students like it because they don't have to wait a long time for feedback and because they have the chance to learn from each other's performance successes and failures as well as their own. Tutors like it because it is quick and they can avoid carrying heavy piles of marking around. However, if it is to be successful, it must be meticulously prepared. Most of the effort is front-loaded, in that the work takes place before rather than after the student performance. Assessment by poster display is widely used in a variety of disciplines.

Why use poster assessment?

Poster displays can be a really useful way by which students can be assessed within a teaching situation. Commonly, students are set a task, either as individuals or in groups, which would normally have as an outcome some kind of written report. Instead they are asked to display their findings, usually as a single A1 sheet, which in the case of a small activity may simply be on flipchart paper, but for more complex tasks could be provided on good quality card and incorporate text, photographs, graphs and so on. Because space is limited, students are required to condense their findings to fit the available space, but our experience shows that the groundwork and preparation have to be as extensive as for a full-length report. It is an excellent skill for students to achieve to be able to summarize complex material into an easily assimilable form, and also provides students from all disciplines with an opportunity to develop visual and layout skills, which are beneficial in all kinds of areas.

It is fast and easy for staff to mark, as they can use a checklist of previously agreed criteria against which to assess the poster. We have seen it work best when students are involved in the peer assessment of each other's work. Typically, students will be involved in the negotiation of the criteria for assessment, which are then shared within the group. After the posters have been produced, students view each other's work and are able to comment and assess using a checklist derived from the negotiated criteria. If anonymity is required, students can be split into two groups and asked to assess posters prepared by the other half.

A major benefit of this approach is that students have an understanding and knowledge of how other students have tackled the task, rather than it being a matter just between the tutor and the individual student, as it often is with traditional assessment methods. At the University of Northumbria at Newcastle, this method has been used to great effect with, for example, mechanical engineering degree students with a design problem and HND medical laboratory technician students researching dietary fats and their effect on human health, where they have presented poster summaries for assessment purposes.

PEER ASSESSMENT
OF POSTER DISPLAYS

Please assess each of the other group's poster displays. You will need an assessment sheet for each poster. Collectively discuss and assess each poster display according to the following criteria and arrive at a numerical mark for each one. These will then be totalled and an award made.

Number of group being assessed:

Number of group doing the assessment:

Solution
Does the poster suggest a viable, effective and useful strategy to cope with the problem?

1 2 3 4 5 6 7 8 9 10

Please circle the appropriate grade

Visual Impact
Was the poster attractive, striking, self-explanatory, creative, effective and neat?

1 2 3 4 5 6 7 8 9 10

Please circle the appropriate grade

Total marks awarded (out of 20):

Figure 7.1 *Peer assessment of poster displays*

Introducing poster assessment

In the briefing period, students will need considerable support in addressing a new assessment methodology. A useful starting point is to use the Blue Peter 'Now here's one I made earlier' system. Students have the opportunity to see examples of previous students' posters and to critique them in groups.

Obviously the first time you attempt this you may need to make two or three mock-ups for the occasion. Giving yourself the task of actually making a good, bad and middling poster to show the students what you are after certainly helps to sharpen up your own criteria for success.

Given the simple questions, 'Which of these are good and which are bad? What makes them that way?', students can discuss the criteria necessary for assessing poster displays. The tutor can participate actively in the plenary. Indicating the weighting to be given to particular criteria, such as whether the visual attractiveness of the poster is a major or minor element of the process, can be open to student negotiation. In any case, it is essential that students leave the session ready to produce their own posters with clear knowledge of what is required.

Whether the assessment is by staff, peers or both, it will be necessary to organize a display of posters for assessment. At the University of Northumbria, these are often arranged in public places, such as the main foyer of a building, so that others can have the chance of seeing what students can achieve. Exhibitions of posters in a public place can demonstrate students' competence to visitors, tutors and students on other courses. The assessment can take place at crucial times, such as during the visit of the external examiner or at open days, thereby serving a secondary PR function as well.

Orals and vivas

Orals and vivas have been part of the traditional repertoire of assessment in universities for years. They have the advantages of immediacy, of enabling assessment to be done in class, of enabling the individuality of students to show through; and there is the added advantage that it is difficult to cheat in a viva. However, vivas and orals are very time-consuming to stage, as they are normally done on a one-to-one basis or in small groups. Staff on language courses often report that teaching time is steadily being eroded by the need to provide sufficient assessment time as class sizes increase.

Increasingly, vivas are used as a kind of quality check. Where, for example, a group has worked on a project with a single output such as a group report or portfolio, vivas make it possible to get a feel for how great a responsibility each person has taken (see also the section on peer assessment in Chapter 5). Similarly, a tutor may take a quality assurance role in peer assessed work by interviewing at random perhaps 20 per cent of teams. Otherwise the tutor may choose to viva those groups who are exceptionally good, exceptionally bad or on the borderline.

Mini-enterprises

These are a special version of problem-working activities, including design and build work. Mini-enterprises are most appropriate to programmes which are engaging students on aspects of commercial life. We are including aspects of public sector activity there, since it is increasingly a sector which is exposed to commercial pressures.

It is commercial pressures and practices that are the principle focus of mini-enterprises. In essence students form an organization, the mini-enterprise. School students have for years had the opportunity of being members of Young Enterprise. Here the student volunteers form small companies, taking and selling shares in their company in order to raise operational capital. They also take on roles within the company – production workers, company secretary, finance director, sales manager, for example. They decide upon a product or range, design, make and sell it (or it may be a service which is being sold), winding the company up at the end of a school year, and paying a final dividend to the shareholders, if a final dividend has been earned.

These mini-enterprises are a realistic way of teaching about the organization of commerce, but they also show the importance of working in and leading teams; of market research; of the economics of making something or providing a service; and of the business of selling. At the University of Northumbria at Newcastle, during Alternative Learning Week, students organized and ran a wine-importing company, subsidizing their buying trip with profits from sales.

Such activities have obvious potential for students in marketing but the aim of teaching about the organization and running of business is also of value to accountants, lawyers, engineers, pharmacy students and the like. The problem is that these mini-enterprises are very time-consuming, and share many of the problems identified with design and build assessment. The range of students for whom these activities are so important that they ought to be provided is relatively small.

It should be remembered, though, that a number of students are involved in 'mini-enterprises', most notably through Students' Unions. Others are involved in mini-enterprises simply to survive, selling fudge, second-hand clothes/books/records, providing catering/secretarial/tutorial services, and so on. We are not proposing that these 'extra-mural' activities should be assessed, but we do think that it is in students' interests for them to be documented, probably through their Record of Achievement. We are aware that BTEC courses encourage claims from learners that they have acquired competence in common skills through activities outside the learning environment. Accreditation of Prior Learning may, in some cases, work in the same way.

This usefully reminds us that the experience of being a student is much greater than what academics see through their contact with students. Some of that experience is best not documented, other parts might be lucrative if documented under a pseudonym, but still other parts attest to achievements which the university courses may have by-passed.

Fieldwork and lab work

Fieldwork has been a very widely used component of many degree courses in, for example, the biological sciences, in geography and in construction courses. Very often a great deal of learning goes on during fieldwork that is normally beyond the scope of assessment. This may include not only learning that takes place within the subject discipline but also learning within the domain of transferable skills to do with teamwork, groupwork, negotiated learning, learning from practical experience and so forth.

Assessment of such learning can be problematic, because so much of it is *ad hoc* and informal. However, increasingly courses are requiring students on fieldwork to keep detailed learning logs or activity logs and these can form part of an assessment component either submitted as a written assignment, or used as the quarry from which material for a presentation or a project can be offered at a later stage.

It is a good idea not to restrict the assessment to written instruments; for example, students can be encouraged to use portable tape recorders, video cameras and photographic recording of achievement which can later be used as part of a portfolio of learning achievement during fieldwork. The least appropriate form of assessment for fieldwork seems to be exam questions, although they can be used creatively so that learners can demonstrate their learning from fieldwork and in particular can be asked to reflect on the achievements that have taken place during such experiences, particularly in terms of communication, groupwork and leadership.

Portfolios

In disciplines such as fine art where text is less important than image, assessment is largely through a collection of artefacts included within a portfolio (literally, 'a collection of pages'). Increasingly other disciplines are adopting the methodology so as to enable students to use a range of non-text media to demonstrate their abilities. Such portfolios might take the form of a box file which includes a range of documents such as sample course work, reports, correspondence, minutes of meetings, etc., but also perhaps video and audio tapes of interviews or negotiations, computer print-outs, spreadsheets and graphic material. In fact, there is in theory no restriction as to what may be included in a portfolio.

However, learners need careful briefing to ensure that they don't just include everything that comes to hand. A portfolio is not a heap of material, and there is a case for saying that the grade that is awarded has as much to do with the selection and the learner's explanation of that selection as it does with the actual content of the portfolio. We could say that students need self-awareness if they are to give of their best in portfolio assessment. So, the key terms are selection, range and progression. A portfolio that contains too much will be exceedingly bulky and impossibly time-consuming to mark. Students will need guidance about choosing what they put into their portfolio so that it shows the best of what they can do over a wide range of material and demonstrates improvement over a period of time. A limit on volume can be imposed by allowing only a single box file or an artist's A1 portfolio to contain the materials. Anything too bulky to fit in can be represented by photographs or videotapes (this is, for example, how sculptors are able to demonstrate their oeuvre without having to transport bulky artefacts).

Another essential element of the portfolio is, we believe, a critical account of the contents – more than an annotated contents list – which provides an opportunity for the student to contextualize the work and demonstrate the learning achieved.

Artefacts/products

In many areas, the best evidence to demonstrate students' competence is something that has been made as part of the learning process. For creative artists this may be, for example, a sculpture, a garment, an item of ceramics or an installation. For an engineering student, it may be a robot, something turned on a lathe, or a vehicle. For students of hotel and catering studies, it may be a table setting, an item of food or a whole meal.

In many cases the artefact will be available for assessment, but it may, like a gateau or a leaf sculpture, be ephemeral, and it may involve quite a strong element of personal taste (gastronomic or aesthetic). Fairness and validity of assessment will depend heavily on clear and overt criteria, either supplied or negotiated, and a recognition that, unlike many forms of written assessment, there are unclear lines between right and wrong. Assessors will need to guarantee equivalence of experience of assessment rather than identicality, and ensure that dependence on experience in matters of judgement is tempered with objectivity.

Designs, drawings and plans

Assessment of this kind can provide an opportunity for public assessment, as in the case of poster displays, and this is an opportunity that is frequently missed. Assessment of exhibitions, models, drawings and so on can be made open to a variety of agencies. For example, a perfect opportunity is provided for employers, the general public, fellow tutors, the students' own peers, to be involved in the assessment of such product and, indeed, very often it's a great waste that the productions that students put so much energy and effort into achieving are often only seen by a very limited audience.

At the University of Northumbria, where models are often used in assessments on the building management degree, these are made available to quite a wide variety of people, and as many as possible are involved in the assessment, in order to provide students with an opportunity to make assessment a celebratory occasion and not just a private process between the tutor and lecturer.

Of course, where more than one individual is involved in assessing any assignment, it is necessary for explicit criteria to be made available and a proforma or mark sheet of some kind to be used, so that there is reliability across the assessors. However, in this way the assessment exercise becomes an active rather than a passive one, and provides learning opportunities not just for the individual or small group of peers who may have been involved in its production.

Design and build

This is a special case of problem-working activities. Design and build (D and B) activities are well suited to those professions in which what matters is the production of 'semi-solutions' that work: engineering comes to mind, but any programme in which an outcome would be a working resolution of a situation which needs the creation of an artefact would lend itself to design and build assessment. Examples include teaching (provision of curriculum materials), theatre studies (construction of a set), electronics, architecture (on a cheap scale, naturally), agricultural science and software engineering.

Above all, D and B assessment is time-consuming, stressful for students and often for their supervisors too: there are many uncontrolled variables, which may be lifelike, but which also make for uncertainty in assessment. Validity has been raised at the expense of reliability, and that takes us back to the discussion in Chapter 2 of assessing competence. It is neither cheap nor easy and it's not possible to predict what the assessment task will actually demand of the learner. Moreover, the amount of time that they take means that it is not possible to raise reliability by setting many D and B problems, since there just isn't the time. A solution, already used in medicine, is to computerize the D and B problem. This has several disadvantages, not the least being that it involves framing the problem for the learner and does not require any display of the important practical ability to build the thing. The task has ceased to become D and B and is now a simulation activity or a problem-working task.

In addition, there is the professions' traditional high regard for displays of extensive knowledge and understanding, pure and simple. Therein lies another problem with D and B assessment, that it often does not lend itself to a graded solution. Traditional degrees are classified and we look to fix a mark on any assessment item. It is not only D and B assessments that provide the assessor with problems in this respect, but it is the case that with many D and B assessments one can say little more than that the task criteria have been met and that competence, as defined, has been shown. Finer grading is not generally possible.

These are high-validity ways of assessing, at considerable time cost, a range of achievements associated with the knowledge of quite a limited part of the curriculum. They lend themselves well to formative purposes, hence to self- and peer assessment. They do not, though, sit too easily with a number of assumptions about HE. If D and B tasks are to be used for summative assessment then it would be prudent to consider how many different achievements might be assessed through one project – current assumptions that one task assesses one outcome need to be replaced, and not just with D and B activities.

Games and simulations

Games and simulations are widely used in HE nowadays, often to let students experience situations and occurrences that do not form part of their normal learning experiences.

Law students at the University of Northumbria at Newcastle, for example, take part in a game set in a post-holocaust spaceship where they need to establish collectively the basis of the laws of the society in which they live. This requires them to put on one side all their previous conceptions about law and to go back to basic principles about the purposes and values of law-making. Such an exercise can be assessed (this particular one isn't, as it forms part of induction) if there is a need to assess, for example, transferable personal skills. Elsewhere in the course, simulations of negotiations and court activity are assessed as part of the necessity to provide law students with a grounding in legal skills that have in the past been acquired informally.

Many subjects provide a context in which simulation can be used for assessment. At the University of Northumbria at Newcastle, for example, surveying students are assessed on how they undertake negotiations between a client and a housing association for the lease of premises. Local professionals are involved in the setting of the assignment, using actual local properties and, when possible, role-play themselves, before contributing to the students' assessment.

IT-based work

Computers have been used for assessment for a considerable period of time. At first they were most widely used to speed up the marking of multiple-choice assignments, and there is still a valuable role that can be played by computers in this kind of work. Optical mark scanners can, for example, read batches of 3,000 forms in an hour and can produce graphs that not only sort and rank student achievement but can also provide detailed data on the effectiveness of the questions and on the take-up of correct answers and distracters, enabling improved questionnaire design. Some departments have followed through the logic of optical scanners to integrate student registrations, course lists, examination lists, marking, results analysis and presentation, leading through to the preparation of references.

Computers can be used effectively to generate multiple variations on questions that are numerically based. In engineering questions where students are asked to calculate from a set of variables, the variables and solutions to the problems can be generated by the computer, so that, if necessary, each student can be provided with a slightly different set of problems to answer. The exam, its resit and next year's exam can all be produced at the same time. This can be time-saving and can also help combat some of the problems of plagiarism experienced with students being tested on computer systems.

Perhaps most excitingly, computer networks can be used for assessments, with the tutor able to review and moderate students' performance on-line. This can be valuable for distance learning, for widening access to disabled students and also to permit the use of computer systems on open access outside of normal hours, because the tutor can respond to student inputs either simultaneously or at a later stage, picking up work that has been down-loaded to him or her at the most suitable times.

At the University of Northumbria at Newcastle, a colleague teaching first-year sociology developed a set of computer tutorials to complement the first-year lectures. His original aim was simply to develop in the students a grounding in IT skills but, having toyed with the idea of producing computer questionnaires on, for example, the best pubs in Newcastle, he chose instead to produce brief tutorials to reinforce learning from lectures. The pay-off was much greater than he expected, because not only did he find that the tutorials helped students to learn, they also gave him a lot of unexpected data. At its simplest, as Table 7.1 shows, computer-assisted tracking of marks is one way of displaying them so that patterns may be detected. More significantly, when a suitable spreadsheet is applied, it also allows underlying patterns to be detected through simple statistical analysis.

Lecture number:	1	2	3	4	5	6	7
Student:							
A	56	58	12	48	56	60	55
B	71	83	35	0	0	0	0
C	32	21	8	77	83	75	70
D	70	76	45	77	83	75	70
E	0	0	0	0	0	0	0
F	35	37	24	38	44	47	55
G	65	0	62	0	54	0	41

Table 7.1 *Print-out of course marks*

Quite a number of things can be deduced from this set of marks. For example, is student E actually on the course? Tutors waste a lot of time looking for marks of students who either never enrolled or who leave very early on. A print-off like this helps tutors know where to concentrate their efforts. We suggest that there is little to worry about with students A, D and F, although we might wonder what the relationship is between D and C. C was doing pretty badly until week four, after which C's marks became identical with D's. Is cheating going on? G obviously also has problems and is steadily deteriorating; does G have a part-time job alternate weeks, or is this a tutorial slot that suffers from high-rail-fares-on-Friday blight? B obviously suffered a set-back in week three and may well have lost heart. It certainly needs investigation. So, too, does what happened in week three. Why did everyone do so badly? Was the tutorial particularly hard, or was the material badly taught, or what? It came as an added bonus that this kind of feedback became available as a by-product of using computer tutorials.

A major problem that has been highlighted is the potential for students to plagiarize or cheat on tutorial assessments. It has to be recognized that a really determined computer-literate student will be able to evade all the normal controls and passwords. Therefore assessment by computer tutorials will either have to be used for feedback rather than summative marks, or the system will have to be backed up with, for example, occasional random or targeted viva.

At Lancaster there is teaching by computer conferencing. The examination of one of these courses was individualized, with students each selecting in advance quotations from the conference which interested them. These, along with quotations selected by the tutor, were made up into examination papers in which students had to compare one pair of quotations and contrast the other pair. The examination was not done on-line.

Details of software to support computer-assisted assessment are to be found in the directory published by Guildford Education Services (1993).

Assessment on the page or on the screen – multiple choice

Which of the following statements are true?

- Multiple-choice questions test factual recall only.
- Multiple-choice questions have to be closed in their format.
- Multiple-choice questions are most appropriate in science subjects.
- Multiple-choice questions are unfair since a student can do well simply by guessing.
- Multiple-choice questions are easy to write.
- Academics ought to question assumptions.

About few aspects of assessment is there more confusion than about multiple choice questions (MCQs).

Their advantages are many and quite obvious. A lot of ground can be quickly and easily covered, which is good for reliability and for discouraging students from reducing the curriculum to that fraction on which they might write examination essays. MCQs are easy to mark and it can be done by optical bar-code readers, which means that rapid feedback can be given to students. Computer-based marking also gives the department better records of what students do and do not know and makes it easier to identify major areas for attention.

As medical professors have shown, there is no reason why MCQs should test factual knowledge only. A typical MCQ might comprise a brief description of a patient and presenting symptoms, with the student having to select the most appropriate prescription from a selection of several. Several of the alternatives may be acceptable, and experts may have agreed that one of them is the best and should get more marks than another two, say. The rest, being inappropriate, would score no marks or negative marks. It is possible to see how MCQs could be used in other areas to test understanding: identifying corollaries of scientific principles, the most likely effects of given variation in an organism's environment, the validity of syllogisms, the strength of conclusions which might be made from historical sources, or the match between a set of political principles and a series of political beliefs.

The main problem with MCQs is that they are beasts to write. Andresen *et al.* (1993) mention an estimate that the development time is such that it would take three years before a course with 50 students a year was showing a saving in staff time. Part of that time may come from mistaken beliefs about the design of MCQs: a three-choice MCQ can be every bit as powerful as a five-choice one, which makes it a lot easier to write, yet if reliability is at a premium then many rewrites and plentiful piloting are needed. Moreover, a department will want to build up a substantial bank of MCQs so that a cohort of students gets a different item on a topic than did the students in the past two years. This is not easy, as will become clear if you think of a topic you teach and then try to devise three equally-hard MCQs on it. The common requirement that a bank of MCQs cover all the main areas of a course exacerbates the problem.

Plainly one answer is to use MCQs for formative purposes, to be used in peer and self-assessment, perhaps with computer or tutor support. The items still have to be written (but couldn't one cohort of students write questions for their successors? And couldn't they be graded on the quality of the MCQs they wrote?), but the reliability issue wanes. There will still be a validity issue, since in most undergraduate courses there will be aims which are best not approached through MCQs. There is also the matter of guesswork. Plainly, if one is given a choice of three answers, one of which is right, then there is a 33 per cent chance of picking the right answer. In principle it is possible for a monkey with a pin to get a first. On average that will not happen, and an overall mark of 33 per cent (20 per cent if there are five options) is not likely to cause much concern. However, unease about the exceptions has led to systems which are designed to discourage guessing, especially penalty marking. Each wrong answer leads to marks being lost. A rational student who is not sure of the answer to a question will therefore not answer it, incurring no penalty and getting no bonus from 'chance'.

A more interesting point, in our view, is that MCQs test 'receptive' rather than 'spontaneous' knowledge, and receptive knowledge always looks to be more substantial than spontaneous knowledge does. If asked what the principal implications of the theory of relativity are, people may be in greater difficulty than if given a list of five from which they have to choose three.

If an MCQ paper is diagnostic this phenomenon is not so important. The student who cheats here is a dunderhead. Misguided, but more subtly so, is the student who mistakes good performance on MCQs as a harbinger of good performance where spontaneous knowledge has to be shown. The doctor who can recognize contra-indications of the triple childhood vaccination is dangerous if she or he does not also have the spontaneous knowledge of those contra-indications.

Seen as a part of an overall strategy of assessment, MCQs have a great deal to commend them. Alone, they are limited and time-consuming, although still especially worthwhile in some disciplines. Taken in conjunction with other methods used for other purposes, they have great power.

Assessing workplace learning

Placements

Nationally, there are several programmes looking at ways in which to accredit the learning that takes place in the workplace. These initiatives look at learning both as part of a recognized university course, as with the Accreditation of Work Based Learning (AWBL) programme at the University of Northumbria at Newcastle, and as free-standing units of accredited learning which can be CATs credited in a more flexible way, as with the partnership programme at the University of Portsmouth. Essentially such programmes aim to give recognition to the fact that a great deal of learning is taking place outside the university environment.

In the past placements often were not assessed; learning was often assumed to have taken place but not specifically accredited. It was often assumed that although this was the most important part of the course, other than a work diary or log, there was normally little in the way of assessment of the learning involved. The move towards competence-based learning has altered this, for example in the way in which quantity surveying students at the University of Northumbria at Newcastle are expected to demonstrate a significant and extensive set of competences in their sandwich year out. Instead of theory being divorced from practice, with the course providing the theory and the workplace providing the opportunities to put it into practice, they are seen more holistically, with theoretical and practical elements being joined as praxis.

Commonly a learning contract will be employed to accredit workplace learning. On a placement this is usually best negotiated after a brief induction period, so that appropriate learning outcomes can be identified. Students can then collect evidence over a period of time, which would be verified by the workplace supervisor/mentor against agreed standards.

Learning contracts

Why use them?

Learning contracts are being very widely used throughout HE nowadays, because they are so flexible and they provide a great deal of autonomy and independence in students' assessment.

It is valuable to have procedures which enable an assessment to be made of students' competences on entry and which then enable them to build up individual learning programmes, so that they do not have to repeat elements they have already achieved, and so that gaps in their learning can be successfully dealt with. These procedures can also be profitably used to orient a period of work placement.

Learning contracts tend to stretch students because they depend entirely on the students' own abilities and competences on entry and include ipsative development, that is, development in relation to the students themselves.

Using learning contracts can be very valuable in the context of accreditation of work-based learning and in accrediting prior experiential learning.

How do learning contracts work?

Learning contracts can be as simple or as complex as the assignment task requires. Small-scale learning contracts may take place over a very short period, whereas larger scale learning contracts can be used over a whole semester, a whole year, or indeed, over a whole course.

Generally speaking, there are four basic stages of a learning contract: the skills, knowledge, understanding profile; the needs analysis; action planning and activity; and evaluation. At its simplest the learning contract consists of students identifying with guidance at the beginning of the contract what skills, knowledge and abilities they already have. This can be done through the use of pro-formas or it can be done through one-to-one counselling with tutors, or in small groups of students who help each other to identify their competences.

This having been achieved, the students need to look at the learning outcomes of the course they are undertaking, which will enable them to see the gaps in their own abilities and knowledge. This helps them to produce a needs analysis, and to negotiate a programme of learning tailored to their own personal needs, so that they can move from their original position to a position of competence in relation to the learning outcome. Having analysed their needs, they can put together a programme of activities through the process of action planning, either individually, in small groups or in conjunction with a tutor. Here they will need to identify what they have to do, how they are going to do it, the time-scales in which they are going to undertake these tasks, the rationale behind what they are doing and what support they will need from others (tutors, peers and so on). Having planned their actions, they will then undertake them with support and at the end of this particular stage they will evaluate, both themselves and with the tutor, how successful they have been.

In the simplest learning contract, this will be a linear process, but it is obvious that in more complex processes the learning contract can form a loop. Thus, after an initial evaluation, students will be able to review their own personal skills, knowledge and understanding, review what needs still remain unfilled and revise action plans, having renegotiated the learning contract with the tutor as necessary.

Learning contracts, therefore, can be a valuable, adaptable and flexible assessment tool – see Brown and Baume (1992a; 1992b) and Stephenson and Laycock (1993).

Much energy is currently being expended on developing ways in which mentors and workplace supervisors can be trained to achieve equivalence of verification. Obviously, this requires significant commitment of time and resources on the part of the employer, and appropriate coordination, organization and development opportunities have to be provided by the education institution. A great deal can be gained when mentors/industrial supervisors can be provided with opportunities to meet together to discuss learners' achievements in respect of agreed learning outcomes. Such practice, discussion and moderation are vital if workplace assessment is to be a valid representation of course aims and a reliable estimate of learners' achievements.

Those charged with the responsibility for accrediting learning in the workplace will need to decide whether each outcome is to be assessed on an achieved/not yet achieved basis, or whether grades are to be awarded. It is often feasible, when drawing up the criteria for achievement, to include range statements to indicate the level and extent of achievement that is required. However, as some users of the BTEC Common Skills assessment scheme would agree, range statements can be counter-productive, as they can be seen as restrictive and indicating a common denominator of achievement rather than providing suggestions for what might be achieved. Where time and opportunity allow, it is valuable for the range statements for particular learning outcomes to be negotiated, ideally between learner, workplace mentor and tutor.

We believe that accreditation of work-based learning is likely to increase as a method of defining achievement in institutions of HE, and it will require a considerable shift in culture for both HE and workplace organization if it is to be universally accepted. It has tremendous implications in terms of resourcing and particularly the weighting of payment to institutions and workplaces, but it is a development that is driven both by the Employment Department and by student need, in a climate where full-time study on traditional three-year degree courses is becoming perceived by some as a luxury not all can afford.

Profiles

Profiles are a record of individual students' achievements, usually in terms of statements about a series of competences or learning outcomes. *Profiling* is inherently a formative exercise, enabling the student to continually loop around a cycle of self-evaluation, needs analysis and action planning in order to continuously improve. The involvement of academic staff as advisers, helping learners to identify priorities and means of working towards them, is heightened in a well-devised profiling system. It will be obvious that such developments are not an unmixed blessing, since universities are having to limit the amount of individual attention which students can be given. Furthermore, the spread of modularization and unitization threatens to make it far harder to keep track of students' achievements and make it hard for any tutor to know how best to guide students in the web of options that is now widely available.

A distinction is drawn by Fenwick *et al.* (1992) between occupational *competences* which relate specifically to an occupational area and its functions, and *learning outcomes* which do not have to relate directly to narrowly defined work-related functions, but may include areas of knowledge and transferable intellectual skills. Fenwick and Nixon suggest that this approach has significant implications for modes of assessment:

Profiling requires a shift of perspective towards criterion-referenced assessment: student learning is assessed against clearly stated criteria, in this case, learning outcomes. Once this shift has been made, grading scales which rely on some element of norm referencing begin to appear less appropriate. The focus is on an individual student's development and achievement of their own learning goals and therefore consideration should be taken to ensure that grading scales within profiles, which are used to contribute towards degree awards, do not serve to perpetuate the norm-referenced approach which profiling seeks to move away from (Fenwick and Nixon, 1992, p.3).

NVQs and assessment in HE

Why do we need National Vocational Qualifications (NVQs)? There is a government imperative at the moment to ensure that the workforce is effectively trained in vocational competence. It is determined that at all levels and in all occupations people will be able to demonstrate their capability through workplace assessment of nationally accredited competences at five levels.

The level that first affects HE is Level 3, which is said to be equivalent to A Levels, and increasingly in HE we will see students coming in with NVQs as an entry requirement. Level 4 at NVQ is broadly equivalent to an HND /first degree, and Level 5 is to represent professional competence, which *might* be broadly equivalent to a degree. These are not hard and fast equivalencies, and much debate still exists about them, especially Level 5.

At the time of writing, NVQs are just beginning to be offered extensively in HE but limited to only a few sectors. However, this is due to grow dramatically, as different disciplines come on stream.

While competence at Level 1 requires students to demonstrate fairly limited abilities, competence at Level 5 involves the application of fundamental principles and complex techniques in a wide and unpredictable range of work situations, together with responsibility for other people's work and the allocation of substantial resources. NVQs will be as challenging and demanding as other competences required in HE.

The standards for NVQs are set by the 150 lead bodies which are made up of groups of employer representatives, who therefore have an interest in determining what the Levels of achievement represent. Verification is done by organizations such as RSA, Pitman and City and Guilds who are the awarding bodies, who are then in a position to prepare the different forms of assessment and to establish that candidates can meet those standards.

Assessment of NVQs

A wide variety of methods is used but the emphasis is primarily on candidates showing what they can do rather than traditional assessment methods which look at what candidates cannot do. Assessment methodologies will include practical experience and project assignments as well as more traditional forms of assessment, with the emphasis being on looking for evidence of competence in the workplace.

Those taking NVQs are not graded, they are simply indicated as competent or not competent at a particular learning outcome. You can build up NVQ credits progressively, and build up towards the Level you are achieving. There is no requirement, for example, that Level 1 credits have to be achieved before Level 2. Candidates are able to enter at the Level they feel is appropriate and can build up towards the full competence achievement.

A crucial element of NVQs is that they are assessments of competence; assessments of learning, *not* of teaching, so that it is not absolutely essential to register for a specific course of training in order to achieve these levels of achievement. However, it is necessary that candidates should register at a centre where assessment can take place, for example, an HE institution, or directly through City and Guilds.

There have been discussions with UCCA about the place of NVQs, Records of Achievement and National Records of Vocational Achievement in the university admissions system.

GNVQs

GNVQs are designed to be assessed in educational institutions, not in the workplace; to require evidence of knowledge through written means; and to relate to general, vocational skills, such as communication, personal skills and information technology. In the first instance there are four levels of GNVQ achievement and a GNVQ at Level 3 is to be equivalent to two A Levels. At the time of writing in 1993, GNVQs are available in art and design, business, health and social care, leisure and tourism and manufacturing, but only at Levels 2 and 3. In 1992–3 around 100 GNVQ pilots were underway in schools and colleges, but numbers are expected to swell considerably and quickly.

Assessment for GNVQs will differ from A Levels in that they will assess skills, knowledge and understanding as set in the learning outcomes. Centre assessors in schools and colleges will assess portfolios of evidence and these will be supplemented by direct observation of activities (such as oral communication, group participation and IT skills). Additionally, in some instances there will be external lists for Mandatory Vocational Units, designed to confirm key aspects of knowledge rather than examine new knowledge.

Assessment for GNVQs is likely to be, like that for NVQs, on demand – candidates may put themselves forward for assessment when they feel they are ready (even prior to any formal tuition element). They may also be assessed and reassessed several times without penalty, at the discretion of the assessment centre.

This pattern may well have an influence on HE practice, particularly once Level 4 schemes are in place. GNVQs are more 'HE-friendly' than NVQs because they do not stress workplace assessment and they do require demonstrations of knowledge and understanding.

Records of Achievement

These provide a record in portfolio format of what a student has achieved during a period of learning. They are now widely used in secondary and primary schools. Their wider application in HE is a movement we would applaud, providing as it does a much more meaningful outcome than a bland degree classification grade.

Unlike many traditional forms of assessment, ROAs concentrate on what students can do rather than what they cannot do, and often are produced as a result of the profiling process which has helped to chronicle achievement.

Essentially ROAs should provide students with a summation of the competences they have achieved, including opportunities for self-evaluation and forward thinking for action planning. An indication of the range and level of achievement is normally given as well as clear guidance on the learning outcomes achieved in the process. This will be useful for potential employers as well as to the students themselves and will offer guidance when students are embarking on further study as to what has been achieved and what still remains to be done. The biggest current problems are that their use is patchy, quality assurance procedures for verification and validation are still being developed, and the portfolios can look rather daunting to shell-shocked employers. Some useful discussions of RoAs may be found in Assiter and Shaw (1993).

National Record of Vocational Achievement

Through NVQs, individuals can work towards an NVQ National Record of Vocational Achievement, which is made up of four sections. These are the personal record, which gives the candidate's achievement in education and training, work and leisure time; the action plan, which shows the candidate's achievement target, usually including NVQs and other qualifications; the assessment record, which charts the progress made towards the target set in the action plan and may take the form of a chart or plan; and the certificates, awarded by bodies such as the HE institution or City and Guilds, which show the credits or achievements within the NVQ system or beyond.

Summary

We have by no means exhausted the set of assessment methods which might be used, nor have we exhausted our set of examples – at Lancaster there is a substantial *Assessment Toolkit*, which describes methods in use within the university, including some which we have not included in this section. Newble *et al.* (1993) provide a useful discussion of methods used in the assessment of clinical competence (including the interesting Objective Structured Clinical Examination), and business schools have adopted the not dissimilar idea of assessment centres.

Space has stopped us from discussing the potential for assessment of some useful teaching techniques, such as concept mapping, making flow charts, designing learning aids for others, and marking others' work. Nor have we examined ways of using assessment methods to tell us about the impact of our teaching on *groups* of students, well covered by Angelo and Cross (1993). Similarly, we have avoided the interesting problem of how we assess academics' 'teaching' performance, something which is discussed in the collection edited by Knight (1993).

What we have done, though, is to emphasize that assessment is a many-splendoured thing. Some may wish to do no more than to try out some of the methods that we have described: curriculum theorists are increasingly realizing that this 'tinkering' is an extremely important form of change and not to be derided because it is on a small, human and practicable scale – those are its strengths.

However, we repeat our basic theme, that there is an assessment crisis for universities *as a whole*. Tinkering is admirable, but it will become important to make a difference to the whole system, not least by spreading principles for better assessment. To that we turn in Part 3.

Part 3: Assessing better

Dr. Blind . . . had taught for the past fifty years a course called 'invariant subspaces' which was noted for its monotony and virtual complete unintelligibility, as well as the fact that the final exam, as long as anyone could remember, had consisted of the same single yes-or-no question. The question was three pages long but the answer was always 'yes'. That was all you needed to know to pass 'invariant subspaces' (Donna Tartt, *The Secret History*, 1992).

Put NIH (Not Invented Here) behind you – and learn to copy (with unique adaptation/enhancement) with the best . . . Become a 'learning organization' (Peters, 1989, p.228).

Chapter 8:

Speedier Assessment

A strategic approach to assessment

We develop in Part 4 the idea that we need systemic approaches to assessment. Here we want to begin making that case. As pressures on tutors increase it is necessary for them to adopt a strategic approach to:

- the amount of assessed work they require
- its forms
- when it is required
- submission deadlines
- feedback to learners
- the use of paid markers
- assessing with other tutors.

Feedback

For example, it makes sense to ensure that a lot of feedback is given to students very early on in the process when they are being coached to perform well; as they progress towards the end of a module, when they are well aware of what is required of them, they need less feedback. Where assignments are marked in class, it is possible to give oral feedback there and then, but tutors at Oxford Brookes University, for example, have used audio tapes to give feedback to students.

Amount of assessed work

Sometimes it is possible simply to cut down the number of assignments that are given. Where a unit has been designed with four or five essays, for example, it might be possible to replace one or two of those essays with a combined assignment, or indeed simply to cut back on the number in total. It is a good idea to devise fewer, bigger assignments, which may take the form of small elements which are staged in their handing in, to form a portfolio at the end (see Chapter 7 on portfolios). Consideration must also be given to how much tutors can reasonably be required to read. Most people recognize that it is very difficult to write fluently, articulately and *concisely*, but these are skills that are highly regarded by employers and we would do well, as tutors, to ensure that students are able to do this as part of their degree programme.

If word limits are set, it is a good idea to stick strictly to them. Some students believe that the more they write, the greater number of marks they are likely to achieve, and this has a knock-on effect on tutors, who find they are marking much longer assignments. Where word limits are given it should be made clear to students that anything after this number of words (approximately) will not be read.

Submission procedures

One time-waster is when students hand in work late, or incomplete, or inappropriately formatted. It is a good idea to include such details on the briefing sheet and to be quite strict on late submission of work other than in specified and authenticated circumstances. Some tutors nowadays expect all work to be typewritten or word-processed, and this might be considered quite tough unless IT and text-handling skills are deemed appropriate to the course. In order not to disadvantage students, in addition, this requirement should not be made unless there are sufficient open-access IT facilities. However, there is no doubt that typed or word-processed work is much easier and quicker to mark. Certainly, many tutors for many years have indicated that they will not mark illegible or impossibly badly presented work, because this in itself is time-consuming.

In the University of Northumbria at Newcastle a great deal of staff time has been saved in one of the engineering departments by use of an assignment clerk, provided with funding vired from a small amount of part-time visiting lecturers' budget. The role of the clerk is to collect in all the work from students, to bundle it appropriately and hand it to the person who is to do the marking. The assessor then marks the scripts and hands them back to the clerk, whose responsibility it is to record those marks appropriately and distribute them. This kind of system is most effective when there are large numbers of students because it is at that time that the amount of administration involved in handling students' work becomes greater and more difficult. The funding can be justified because it frees up tutors from a great deal of administrative drudgery so that they can concentrate on what they are employed to do: teaching and assessment.

Assessing with other tutors

Where several tutors share the assessment of assignments from a large group, it is essential that the criteria that tutors are marking to are agreed between them. In the past, reliability has been widely ensured by the use of co-markers and double marking, but we assert that this can be very wasteful of energies and, as student numbers increase, it is very difficult to justify the energy that is expended in double-marking. We would suggest that it might be better for tutors either to share out the marking so that one tutor will assess question one, another question two and so on; or, that tutors should act as quality assurers for each others' marking, sampling each other's work. In this way, particularly when scripts are marked anonymously, tutors would be able to take a pile of scripts at random and mark them separately. So long as the criteria being used are agreed and clearly specified, it should be possible for tutors working in this way to validate each other's work.

Another method that can be used is for tutors to select from their own pile of scripts the best, the worst and a sample of those around the middle range, and to exchange these. This does, at least, ensure some equity in the marking. A third way is for tutors to assess work and rank order it. Negotiation is then possible about rank order and marks can be allocated in bands. Quibbling about individual mark differences can then be avoided, with tutors having freedom to be flexible about numbers being assigned within the bands. What is most wasteful is where tutors argue over a few percentage points. Where co-marking exists, it is quite common for a reasonable degree of consensus to be achieved on band marking, whereas individual number marking can lead to a great number of quibbles.

Assessing less to a good purpose

Many assessment systems have been inherited from prior schemes and often have not been reviewed. We tend to assess what we have always assessed in the way we have always assessed it. This means that, on occasions, we tend to over-assess students; we often assess the same element a number of times. For example, students very often have to write up laboratory reports for each lab they undertake and hand in all those reports. Some tutors maintain this is necessary in order that students have the opportunity to develop the appropriate style for writing up laboratory reports. However, as student numbers have increased, it is relatively common for tutors to tell students to write up all their lab reports, and then either the students themselves select two or three to hand in, or the tutors will at random choose reports which have to be handed in, with the students not knowing which ones will be called for. This is to ensure that all students write up all reports and that students have to write a lot of reports but tutors don't have to review so many. We believe this is wasteful of students' effort and also a waste of the assessment exercise, because students may well write a lot of reports but they don't get the opportunity for formative feedback. Repetitive activity rarely ensures improvement of performance unless feedback is given.

How much better it would be, we suggest, if students were required to write something for each report but not necessarily a full report every time. In some instances, for example, the student might be asked to write simply the introduction and methodology and hand that in. On other occasions, they might be asked to write only the discussion section. It is generally the case that writing a summary or abstract is actually harder than writing a whole report, so towards the end of the process it might be a good idea to ask students to write only the abstract. Later on, during a unit or module it would be useful, perhaps, for the students to write, submit and have assessed a full report, but certainly we do not believe that it is essential that this is done every time.

Similarly, with non-scientific subjects, it is often the case that students are asked to write a very large number of essays for different elements of their courses. In this way, tutors hope to develop students' writing skills, ability to reason and present an argument and their general fluency. However, there is frequently very little liaison between subject elements within degree courses, and so learning from one element is not necessarily transferred to another. It would be better, therefore, for a wider variety of assessment methodologies to be used, with some using essays, some using memorandum reports, book reviews and so on, so that students are using different kinds of writing style in order to achieve the learning outcomes. Indeed, we would argue that the whole range of assessment methods can be used to effect, including assessment methods which enable marking to be done within class time, so that different competences are developed and extended. Notice that we are not saying that students should do less work.

Marking with overt criteria

Why do it?

Making the criteria by which a piece of work is assessed explicit and out in the open is advantageous for a number of reasons. First of all, it seems fairer and more reasonable that students should know what it is they're trying to achieve, rather than these things being secret and hidden within the mind of the marker. It avoids students wasting a lot of time and energy on things that they are not required to do and not putting the time into the things that are important. When students are given, or negotiate, the criteria by which they are to be assessed, they tend to achieve the required outcomes more effectively and they also tend to achieve better results. This means that using overt criteria tends to improve the overall marks of a cohort of students. Where students are criterion-referenced, this is extremely valuable, although where students are norm-referenced, it may be quite startling to markers to find that the overall standard of achievement is higher. However, as we promote a competence-based programme of assessment, we believe that criterion-based marking is fairer than norm-referenced marking.

Who does it?

Basically, where the criteria are overt and explicit, it becomes possible for more people than simply the tutors to mark it. Even when the tutor is marking alone it is helpful to have a detailed and specific mark scheme with the criteria included. It is invaluable to have such a scheme when more than one tutor is marking work, for example, when several tutors mark assessed work from seminars linked to one lecture group. In these cases, it is easier for an agreed standard to be achieved and double-marking can, on occasion, be avoided. It is possible in these cases to sample mark across a shared assessment programme in order to ensure the quality of the marking.

However, we would assert that a prime advantage of using overt criteria, whether imposed upon learners or agreed with them, is that the learners themselves can become involved in assessing their own work (see Chapter 5).

When should it be done?

The most effective time to give the students the criteria by which they will be marked is at the briefing session for the assignment. This can be done at a variety of levels. The lecturer can, for example, simply give a handout to the students or provide an OHP in the lecture session and take the students through what is expected of them. This can be done quite broadly or in great detail, with the marking scheme and the weightings apparent to the students. We say that greatest benefit comes when the students themselves are involved in negotiating the criteria by which they are to be assessed. Some would argue that when the criteria are made as explicit as this, it then becomes problematic because students tend to achieve convergent results rather than divergent results; that is to say, students tend to produce the same kinds of outcomes. We would argue that this is not the case since, although the criteria upon which students are to be judged are the same, the actual results can be as divergent as when criteria are not given. Indeed, students have more opportunity to develop creative and innovative approaches once the criteria are made explicit, because the boundaries of what must be achieved are then made clear and they are free to be flexible within those boundaries.

Another way that overt criteria can be introduced to assessment is by producing assignment return sheets for students. Any assignment return sheet provides opportunities for tutors to save themselves repetitive writing on student scripts, but they are not in any way intended to replace idiosyncratic comment. The example given in Figure 8.1 provides an opportunity for tutors to use space overleaf on a plain sheet, or on a student's own script, to add additional comments. The idea of the assignment return sheet is to provide structured feedback to students as efficiently as possible. Some assignment return sheets have very many more sections than this, but the more sections there are, the more time it takes for tutors to fill them in. If very detailed sheets are used, it is useful for tutors to make it clear that they will not fill in every single section every time because otherwise the completion of these sheets can be very time-consuming.

In this case, five criteria are used: structure, presentation, style, references and sources, and content. Assignment return sheets are extremely varied and other examples can be found in Gibbs *et al.* (1992).

ASSIGNMENT RETURN SHEET

STUDENT'S NAME ....   **DATE SUBMITTED** ....

COURSE..   **TUTOR**..................................

ASSIGNMENT REF NO ....   **MARK ACHIEVED** ....

STRUCTURE

Appropriate length/too long/too short
Sections are balanced/unbalanced

PRESENTATION

Beautifully presented/adequately presented/poorly presented
Word-processing excellent/satisfactory/poor
Tables and figures excellent/adequate/need attention

STYLE

Very fluent/adequate/poorly expressed
Appropriate/excessively formal/too informal/colloquial
Grammar   Spelling   Punctuation   Satisfactory/needs attention

REFERENCES/SOURCES

Correctly/incorrectly referenced
Missing detail =

Other references you might consider

....

CONTENT

Detailed/interesting/appropriate/adequate/insufficient/derivative

Additional tutor comments overleaf.

Figure 8.1 *A sample assignment return sheet*

In the assignment return sheet shown in Figure 8.1 there is a series of alternatives which can be deleted as appropriate and there are also sections for the tutor to add comments on the assignment return sheet as necessary.

Self-assessment using an assignment return sheet

Another development of this is for students themselves to complete a similar assignment return sheet when they hand in their work. This enables them to develop their own self-evaluative powers, it provides a checklist so that they know what they are aiming to achieve themselves when they hand in their work and it provides an opportunity for the tutor to perceive the gaps that exist between a student's own perceptions of their abilities and the tutor's. In this way assessment becomes a genuine learning experience rather than simply a monologue between the tutor and the student.

On a student self-assessment return sheet, the boxes or the layout could be modified so that there is opportunity for the students to say themselves what they think each section is worth, and for tutors then to take much more of the role of a validator or moderator to review students' achievement. The example in Figure 8.2 shows how the sample assignment return sheet can be modified so student self-evaluation can take place at the point of handing in. Of course, this requires fairly sophisticated abilities by the learner and probably is not a suitable methodology for very early on in the student's learning process. We would suggest it is possible to build progressively towards students' abilities to self-evaluate. In the first instance, criteria should be given by the tutors in relation to each assignment. When the students then have a good idea of what is expected of them, they themselves can be involved in negotiating the criteria and they can go on to negotiate a weighting that each criterion should be given. Ultimately, they should have the competence to review their own work against the set criteria and to self-evaluate their own work effectively, with the tutor having the opportunity to have an overview of achievement and confirm or negotiate on the final grade.

Statement banks

Although tutors believe that when they are assessing students' work they are treating each student as an individual, in many cases most tutors have in their heads a series of comments that they use on numerous occasions. We would term these a 'statement bank' and we would suggest it is possible to use such a statement bank in order to make assessment more efficient. The simplest way, what we would call the 'lo-tech' way, is for the tutor, when marking assignments, to keep a running comments sheet either on paper or an OHP transparency. Every time they want to write a comment on a student's work, they put a numbered asterisk on the script and then put the actual comment either on paper or on the OHP transparency. Student A will have comments 1,2,3,4 and 5 (only the numbered asterisks will appear in their work), Student B may have comments 2,3,5,7, 8 and so on. Thus, an entire bank of statements is built up on paper or on an OHP transparency. When the entire set of scripts has been completed, there may be as many as 20 or 30 comments that apply to the whole cohort of students, although not all students will have the same asterisk numbers on their scripts.

STUDENT'S SELF-EVALUATION SHEET

STUDENT'S NAME ....   **DATE SUBMITTED** ....

COURSE..   **TUTOR**.................................

ASSIGNMENT REF NO ....

STUDENT COMMENT..

TUTOR COMMENT..

STRUCTURE

Appropriate length/too long/too short
Sections are balanced/unbalanced

PRESENTATION

Beautifully presented/adequately presented/poorly presented
Word-processing excellent/satisfactory/poor
Tables and figures excellent/adequate/need attention

STYLE

Very fluent/adequate/poorly expressed
Appropriate/excessively formal/too informal/colloquial
Grammar   Spelling   Punctuation   Satisfactory/ needs attention

REFERENCES/SOURCES

Correctly/incorrectly referenced
Missing detail =

Other references you might consider
....

CONTENT

Detailed/interesting/appropriate/adequate/insufficient/derivative

STUDENT SUGGESTED GRADE ..... **TUTOR MODERATED GRADE** .....
WHAT I WOULD NEED TO DO TO THIS ASSIGNMENT TO ACHIEVE A HIGHER GRADE:

Figure 8.2 *A sample assignment return sheet modified for student self-evaluation*

When returning work, either the statement bank with the appropriate numbered asterisks indicated can either be put up on an OHP transparency at the beginning of a lecture, or a copy of the comments can be circulated to all students. Learners can then be advised to cross-reference the asterisk numbers to their own work and, in the lecture, for example, learners be told that they should look at the numbers on their scripts and the comments that appear on the OHP. If they are unlikely to remember the comments they should then write them directly on their scripts, otherwise they should read, mark and inwardly digest. If, instead, the statement bank is on paper, over a period of time a large number of statements will be collected and these can form a typed, photocopied sheet that can be stapled on top of students' work and the appropriate comments ticked.

This may sound very impersonal, and some tutors are very resistant to using a method like this because they feel it removes the possibility of individual comment. We would not suggest in any way that this should be the case. Where idiosyncratic comment is needed, this can go directly onto the individual student's work, but we would assert that the vast majority of words that are written on students' scripts are written again and again by tutors. This system is to eliminate some of that repetition.

One way to get together a paper statement bank is to look through a pile of scripts you have marked previously and to copy them from that pile of scripts, either yourself or using administrative support, and make up a typed list of statements. Some tutors worry that learners will not like this methodology but our experience shows that they prefer a slightly more mechanistic approach that gives them a lot of information on what they have achieved, to the very minimal approach that some tutors are being forced to adopt as the number of students increases. We ourselves have noticed that the amount of feedback we have been able to give students has dropped over the years.

A 'hi-tech' method of using statement banks is to have all those statements on disk on computer and to note simply which statements will apply to an individual script. These can then be pulled up on screen and printed out as appropriate. This is a methodology that is used very widely in preparing school reports.

Our preference is, however, for a medium- or lo-tech version, because at least it acknowledges that a statement bank is being used, where the on-disk version can look as if it is trying to pretend it isn't.

Using marking schemes

When devising marking schemes, it is important to review critically what the assessment is trying to achieve. To adapt a Marxist principle, 'If it don't work, it don't eat', that is to say, if the assessment is not doing what it is supposed to be doing, then it doesn't belong within the assessment system. So, when devising a marking scheme, tutors should be looking very carefully at what it is they want students to be able to do or to know, or what competences they are looking for, prior to setting the assignment. All too often the assignment or essay question is set and the mark scheme not devised until a later stage. This is putting the cart before the horse, because learners will quite carefully apportion their efforts in direct proportion to the marking schemes. This provides us with an opportunity to direct student energy into those areas that we think most important and it also gives us a possibility to consider carefully whether we need to assess every element in each assessment.

When assessment is formative then it is worth putting a lot of energy into it, so that the assessment becomes an integral part of the learning process. In this case, it is necessary to use a large amount of feedback which will enable students to improve their performance. Where assessment is summative only, that is, it is end-point and purely about letting students know whether they have or have not achieved a required standard, then we would assert that there needs to be very little in the way of text and that concentration should be on numbers instead.

Assessment schemes should have a system whereby the importance we place on any particular element is matched by the weighting within the assessment system. Where more than one person is to mark, it is invaluable for each participant to be involved in designing the assessment system, because in that process of deciding the system, differences in point of view between assessors can be discussed and some consensus achieved. This is as much the case when students themselves are involved in assessing work as it is when tutors are to assess work separately or collaboratively.

Giving productive and constructive feedback

In Chapter 1 we identified feedback as a vital element in the learning and assessment process. We also placed a lot of emphasis on formative assessment, the usefulness of which is *entirely* dependent on the quality of feedback. We suggested that it would be helpful if there could be discussion of summative assessments with students, so that they could learn from them. We had in mind the case of Year 2 examinations, which, although they are summative, could be analysed in order to help learners to work towards better performance in their Year 3 examinations. In short, we said that feedback is a crucial part of effective assessment. Students (265 of them) surveyed by a team at the University of Central England (Mazelan *et al.*, 1993) ranked receiving feedback on assessed work as the third most important activity for effective study and as the fifth most important activity for enhancing well-being. So, arguably the important part of assessment does not end when the work has been marked; rather, that is when it begins.

Feedback and approaches to learning

Yet we also reviewed Turner's work on feedback, which showed that students differ in what they want. Some are looking for a few 'global' pointers on how to improve their work and react poorly to detailed comments festooning their work. After all, they say, what value is there in detailed comments on a specific essay that has been finished and which will never be recreated? Others, however, see value in these comments, reckoning that they can amend their understanding of the topic in the light of the tutor's observations. This range of reactions might have been predicted from work on learning styles.

It has been argued that students tend to adopt one of four approaches to learning. The categorization is a little arbitrary and there is no doubt that there are other ways of categorizing approaches to learning. Nor should it be assumed that these approaches are enormously stable; indeed, the whole idea of learning is dedicated to moving students from less to more satisfactory approaches to learning. Yet this set is analytically useful. Entwistle (1993) identifies 'deep', 'surface', 'strategic' and 'apathetic' approaches.

The *deep* approach is characterized by an intention to understand the material, which involves relating ideas, re-working the material into a form that makes sense to the learner, and drawing upon evidence to test them. We might characterize the deep learner as mentally active: certainly such a learner takes an active interest in his or her work – the model student.

The *surface* approach centres on an intention to reproduce the material to be learned. In this sense learning is passive, with the student cast as an assimilator, not as the meaning-maker of the active approach. Fear of failure looms large, while memorization is the prime academic tool.

The *strategic* approach involves cue-consciousness. The student is looking to excel (as are most students) but has decided that the way of excelling varies from course to course and that the main thing is to find out exactly what one is expected to do in order to get good grades in this course or that. It may involve taking a deep approach or it may not. Students who got first class degrees (Arksey, 1992) have reported taking a strategic approach, taking care to 'suss out the system'. Associated with the strategic approach are good time management and an organized approach to study.

The *apathetic* approach is a little uncharitably named, since it not only includes those students who have drifted into HE and who have little interest in the academic side of university life, but also those poor souls who are clueless. A lack of interest is characteristic of this approach (but which of us hasn't been deeply uninterested in some of our studies?) and a lack of direction.

It is quite easy to see how the different approaches could be associated with different attitudes to feedback, as Table 8.1 suggests.

Learning approach	Appropriate feedback
Deep	Detailed comments on the ideas, evidence and techniques. The goal is understanding and feedback should reflect it.
Surface	General comments. The relevance of detailed comments will not be seen.
Strategic	Mark-related comments, cueing students into what they need to do to get better marks. Detailed comments on ideas not welcome.
Apathetic	Encouraging comments needed – but 'boot in the rear' comments *might* 'kick start' the learner. Confidence-building is generally preferred.

Table 8.1 *Learning approaches and feedback*

The main implication of this analysis is that in the ideal world the tutor would have some notion of the style that each learner preferred and would tailor feedback accordingly. It is generally unrealistic to expect this to happen in normal classes, where there are too many students who meet the tutor for too little time. However, the system of academic advisers should embrace these insights and attempts should be made there to match feedback and the learner's preferred approach to learning.

On what should students get feedback?

Obviously, tutors will identify mistakes and errors in students' work. Yet many students, as we have just said, will tend to pay little attention to them, let alone to the implications. If we want learners to revise their existing notes it will usually be necessary to make seminar time and tell them to use their essays to revise, there and then, their notes on a topic. This takes us to seminars at large. There is a sense in which seminars are one of the most powerful and neglected arenas for feedback. Consider a typical routine. The learner attends a lecture on a topic and does (or in the case of apathetic learners, doesn't do) further work in the shape of problems or further reading. A seminar follows. Let us characterize seminars, perhaps rather optimistically, as the thinking part of the course, the lectures being the informing and orienting part. In the thinking part of the course learners will see their ideas being substantiated, challenged or revised. It is seldom made explicit, but there is a strong sense in which seminars are the main form of feedback that students get on topics. The problem is that seldom do students have integrated notes. Lecture notes are filed in one place, reading and problems separately and seminars elsewhere. Some tutors are not sure that learners do make a great deal of use of seminar notes. They may be engaged in the seminar, which may well be lively and stimulating. However, there is doubt as to whether this engagement gets translated into effective feedback, with the insights from the seminar being drawn together and applied to existing knowledge.

Our first recommendation for giving more effective feedback concerns seminar work. From the outset learners should be directed towards producing integrated summaries of topics. These might be a couple of sides of A4 on which learners list key concepts, facts, formulae or proofs. Ideas about their applicability, limits, context and implications would be added. These summaries (which could, of course, be assessed), would draw together information from all sources, including comments on work that has been submitted for assessment. As examinations approach the summaries would be updated. In the humanities and social sciences, an excellent way of updating feedback is for learners to read the book review section of current journals, but often there are revision seminars organized which may have the same effect. In many courses, presentational skills will be assessed and feedback on seminar presentations will be given.

Feedback will also address matters of style. Although this is at a premium in the literary subjects, other subjects also have their conventions that must be followed. Frequently tutors comment upon unsatisfactory features, but this is somewhat eclectic. Departments really ought to have preferred styles into which students are inducted from the beginning. These styles will be set out in the departmental handbook. There are then two main ways of getting feedback on consistency with the set style. The first, preferred, way is for students to check their work themselves. That does mean that there needs to be a departmental checklist, which students complete and submit with their assessed work. This approach is not without its difficulties, for although most people can check accurately whether they have given references in an approved fashion, few poor spellers are very good at checking their own spelling. The same goes for punctuation and grammar. It's not much good asking a student who thinks that Hitler led the Natzis, that a mother defends it's young, that interllectuals are the leaders of society, or that the Russian people was revolting, to assess these facets of the presentational quality of their work. Besides, some students become blasé and end up just ticking everything on a presentational checklist. We recommend, then, that any checklist have two tick columns: one for the learner to complete as self-assessment, and one for the tutor to use if there is disagreement with the learner.

The second approach to giving presentational feedback is for people other than the learner to give it. This could quite easily come from peers but it will generally come from tutors. The main point here is that identifying an area of difficulty is not in itself sufficient. The learner needs to know what the problem looks like, which implies that where tutors identify difficulty they need to explain the nature of the problem. Where the difficulty is that learners cannot spell or have little grasp of grammar, specialist, remedial help will be needed – preferably in the first year.

Ways of giving feedback

This raises the question of what is the best way to give feedback – orally or in writing? In the ideal world we would want to give individual feedback, preferably orally. To explain this we need to draw upon learning theory, which insists that learning is an activity. The learner filters information through the screen of his or her existing knowledge and concepts. This means that effective teaching takes account of what the learner already knows and believes and is reactive to it. Learning, then, is an interplay between the learner and the material to be learned and/or the teacher. It has an element of the esoteric about it, although the eventual product is usually the construction of publicly accepted meanings.

Feedback, ideally, ought to involve the interplay of the tutor's understanding and the learner's. The tutor's task is to shape his or her public knowledge in a way that allows it to mesh with what the tutor has identified as the learner's alternative, insufficient concepts. Dialogue is therefore not simply desirable but, arguably, essential.

Yet such encounters are an impossible luxury in our system. Besides, not all tutors have the sensitivity to hear what the faltering learner is saying; not all faltering learners have the confidence to explain what they (mis)understand; and creating a dialogue that makes a difference requires skill and perhaps training too. We also recall that tutors tend to be people who have soared past conceptual confusion, methodological muddles and prose problems. It is not always easy for them, as experts, to understand why a novice should find difficulty with something that appears to be quite elementary. A useful compromise is to use seminars for group feedback purposes. Tutors can encourage students to group together to identify points on which they want clarification – and in the process groups will tend to explain things to each other, with students providing each other with the feedback they need. It can be useful to have sub-groups list the points they want to raise on question slips, which the tutor may choose to deal with, or which may be farmed out to other sub-groups for attention. Fortified by the group, students can raise points that they would have jibbed at raising individually, and they can find the nerve to say when they still don't understand something. This is also more efficient in terms of the tutor's time than are individual tutorials. In terms of learning theory, the peer interaction is reckoned to be a powerful way of making people examine their own ideas and positions, either in order to defend them or to depict them.

Written feedback will still be the commonest, perhaps because it is the sort of enduring public demonstration that marking has been properly done which examination boards and auditors seek. We have seen that there is no such thing as perfect feedback, with different approaches to learning being associated with different feedback preferences. We have also said that it is desirable for tutors to have a notion of the way problems tend to look to novices so that they can tailor comments appropriately. In other words, giving written feedback is largely an act of judgement, not a science. In addition to the points mentioned earlier, we would say:

- be positive: begin by thanking the student for the work and by mentioning the positive points (there will be exceptions to this adage, but they should be few)
- give two or three powerful pieces of advice as the bulk of the comment – people get bemused by much more than that. This advice should be directed to improving future work and should be phrased as positively as possible
- try to avoid insisting that your view of the answer is the right answer, criticizing learners for reaching alternative conclusions (except where your answer is indubitably the right answer)
- mark points of error in the text of the piece: if possible indicate that there is an error there rather than spell out what it is
- likewise with points where the writer asserts without evidence, puts forward a debatable point of view, becomes rhetorical: indicate with a well-chosen sign, but don't spell it out
- one of the commonest faults in literary subjects is a failure of structure: limp introductions, aimless balks of narrative and conclusions that are as much a surprise as a rabbit coming out of a magician's hat. Advice on structure and organization should be freely given. And given again and again. Seminar time, as we have said, will also be used to reinforce this
- as a final check, ask how these comments are going to help the learner to do better next time. Be especially alert for anodyne suggestions like 'You must work harder'; 'You need to read around the subject'. Try to say what the learner needs to be doing by reading around the subject. What is the harder work to look like?

A useful staff training activity involves practising giving written feedback on these lines, using typed sets of work done by students as the raw materials. Tutors' attempts can be circulated and discussed. The mechanics of setting up comment banks can also be explained in universities where one word-processing package is standard.

Criteria and feedback

The biggest problem is likely to be that tutors typically have multiple criteria that are often poorly articulated. In the words of Sadler (1989, p.126) 'Teachers' concepts of quality are typically held, largely in unarticulated form, inside their heads as tacit knowledge'. He pointed out that at least 50 criteria have been identified for assessing the quality of written composition.

Consequently, we need to insist that worthwhile feedback is related to the clarity of assessment criteria, which we have discussed above. Clearer criteria make for forceful feedback.

It is, unfortunately, a little more complicated than that. Sadler noted that naming a criterion is not the same as understanding it. Students come to understand criteria through experience, through trying themselves out against a criterion and getting feedback. Now we do not want to pursue here the idea that feedback is a necessary part of learning. We want, instead, to suggest that students will be most receptive to feedback related to given criteria if they have already had experience of working with those criteria. One way of doing that is to negotiate criteria with them, but there are some criteria that are given, inherent in the very idea of an honours degree. Becoming aware of the meaning of these criteria might be helped by giving learners tasks like those recommended for staff development, that is, practising applying them to sample pieces of work. Given that both staff and students are in this case learners, it makes sense for them to have similar learning experiences.

We are conscious that this account of giving feedback runs counter to one of the messages of this book, namely that the learner should take increasing responsibility for learning. We see as important the idea of the reflective practitioner, the reflective learner, a person who is becoming better at appraising her or his own performance. The argument set out by Sadler (1989) is that students can be moved from an awareness of the meaning of criteria to increasing peer and self-assessment. There are limits to the degree to which one can assess oneself, but we have already cited evidence that self-assessment is not way out of line with tutor assessment. More importantly, becoming reflective and developing the metacognitive awareness that is a concomitant of becoming an autonomous learner both depend upon becoming more skilled at giving oneself feedback on one's own performance. With this in mind we suggest that learners be required to complete self-assessment sheets for every item of work they do: that is, to give themselves feedback on their own performance. Peter Knight does this on his courses, explaining that the self-assessment can be used to raise a mark by up to 5 per cent, where it is especially perceptive. Non-completion attracts a 5 per cent penalty.

If we had to reduce everything about feedback to one phrase, it would be: create an informed dialogue for improvement. By informed, we do not mean pedantic and pettifogging; by dialogue we do not necessarily mean a verbal interchange; and by development we mean general, wide-scope development. Have a sense of priorities, and in that set of priorities include praise and the positive.

Chapter 9:

Two Issues in Quality Assessment

Mythology

Curriculum change is about changing people (Fullan, 1991). It is their ideas, their beliefs about what is *right*, what *works*, that are being changed: in a sense it is their professional identity and their past practices which are up for reappraisal, which helps to explain why change is no simple business.

Resistance and apathy are normal responses. They may be manifested through a series of academic games (discussed in Chapter 10), but they will certainly involve claiming that the innovation is faulty because it contradicts certain self-evident truths. These truths are often no more than myths, as Gibbs (1991) has argued.

We might construct an alphabet of the best-loved myths, so that:

Z is for Z score, a statistical operation which helps us to compare fairly scores from different tests. The myth is that it is worth using statistical techniques on most assessment data: much is for formative purposes, even more is inherently unreliable and, anyway, people seldom do anything with the lovingly-analysed data. (We do agree that Z scores and their like have their place and value. The problem is that some people imagine that assessment is worthless unless the numbers are hallowed.)

Y is for Yesteryear, the belief that the way in which *we* were assessed put hairs on our intellectual chests, so why should today's students be mollycoddled with 'easier' tests? (In fact, many of the methods described in Part 2 are more demanding than yesteryear's practices. And who wants a hairy chest?)

X is for Xerxes, which reminds us that many colleagues see the main purpose of assessment being to test content knowledge, showing a recall of Xerxes' deeds.

Our first principle for better assessment is that we ought to apply to assessment the same academic flair that we apply to our subjects and recognize and refute assessment myths. Unless they are seen as superstition, large-scale change will not happen.

The meaning of numbers

In that spirit we consider our love of numbers.

Do learners understand what our grades mean? Is *vix satis* (almost satisfactory) a good grade? The next and top grade is *bene*. How does B−− compare to C++ and how many of which do you need if you want to get a 2:2? A mark of 71 may be a first class mark, but if you are doing engineering and your degree class is determined by the mean of your marks on all courses, then it may do you little good unless you also have a solid run of 68. In another department a solid run of 68 would lead to a 2:1, but four 70s and five 60s would lead to a First, even though the mean is 64 per cent.

Strategic students, as is clear from Arksey's book (1992), take care to know what they need to do to win the game. It has to be said that even within the same university the rules vary quite sharply from one department to another, which causes notable aggravation for people taking a combined degree and makes one wonder how universities make judgements about the relative performance of undergraduates in different departments.

Our first point is that the system of using numbers to describe achievement is useless for all purposes except statistical analysis. Since there is little evidence that much statistical analysis takes place this is hardly a compelling reason for cleaving to numbers. Our second point is that unit marks are commonly arrived at by the arbitrary aggregation of marks from different sources. Different rules would produce different results.

If we have gone to the trouble of making clear the aims of a course, and if we have then devised assessments to ascertain the extent to which learners have command of these aims, then the centre of interest is a report on learners' mastery of those goals. Compare the example in Figure 9.1 of better normal practice with an alternative.

Course H201 – Assessment record

Item 1 = 18/30

Item 2 = 15/30

Item 3 = 31/40

Unit coursework score = 64%   *(continues opposite)*

Course H201 – Assessment record

Three assessment items have been completed. On that basis you appear to be able to:

Show that (*insert description of course aim 1 here*) at level two, which means (*insert description of level 2 performance here*).

Understand that (*insert description of course aim 2 here*) at level three, which means (*insert description of level 3 performance here*).

Do (*insert description of course aim 3 here*) at level two, which means (*insert description of level 2 performance here*).

I advise that you choose a module which will give you further practice in (*insert names of aims 1 and 3 here*). Congratulations on (*insert name of aim 2 here*).

Figure 9.1 *Two types of assessment record*

The second form is designed to be computer-based and used with statement banks (see below).

Some have argued that our classification system should be replaced by course transcripts. Those familiar with American transcripts will know that they usually show the Grade Point Average (GPA) for each course taken. A figure of 4.1 is creditable but scarcely tells the reader anything else. Presumably if someone comes along with a GPA of 4.2 they are to be preferred, even though that grade may come from performance on aspects of the programme that we regard as less important than others. Adelman (1990) has exposed the sheer uselessness of many transcripts.

The second problem with numerical assessment of student performance lies in the way unit marks are produced. Most courses involve coursework and examinations. Consider the scenarios given in Figure 9.2.

University of Barchester

Examination mark = 56%

Coursework mark = 63%

Weighting (exam:cw) = 80:20, hence unit mark =57%

University of Telford

Examination mark = 56%

Coursework mark = 63%

Weighting (exam:cw) = 50:50, hence unit mark = 60%, (2:1)

Figure 9.2 *The differential effects of weighting on marks*

Better, we suggest, to report achievement in plain English.

Summary

In this Part we have moved attention away from a concern with methods towards a more strategic interest in policies and principles which support better practices. We need to develop our claim that assessment is a university-wide concern by addressing organizational, management and systems thinking; this we do in Part 4.

Part 4: Assessments and organizations

A costly and demanding triumph of form over substance may well ensue . . . assessment runs the risk of becoming an academic and political debacle (Johnson, 1991, p.111).

Chapter 10:

Focusing on Systems

Innovation in British HE has been common, but this has often been innovation in what was taught, less frequently in how things were taught. So, the geography curriculum has been changed as quantification and generalization replaced the regional studies of the 1930s, while there are now signs that these modelling approaches may themselves be challenged. Likewise, the natural science curricula continue to grow, and it is even rumoured that sometimes topics are deleted as obsolete. Now, while a change from regional geography to quantitative methods, or the adoption of semiotic theory, or the introduction of microcomputer-based statistics packages all clearly mean a change in what is taught, they do carry with them changes in how teaching proceeds. However, our claim is that innovation in teaching, learning and assessment *in their own right* has not been common. Practices may have changed as a by-product of change in what was taught, but they have less often been changed because it was seen as proper that they should change.

Naturally there are exceptions to this claim. There have always been individuals, departments even, who have taught or facilitated learning in ways which were unusual and deliberately chosen. The experiments in the new universities of the 1960s, the foundation of SEDA (Staff and Educational Development Association) and the Enterprise in Higher Education (EHE) initiative all come to mind. While there is no doubt that they have had considerable impact, the reports tend to be of developments in *this* course or in *that* department: little is said about institution-wide change. This can be most starkly illustrated by comparison with Alverno College in Milwaukee, which pioneered institutional approaches to assessment. There, all students are helped to develop in eight cross-curricular areas (communication, analysis, problem-solving, valuing, social interaction, responsibility for the global environment, aesthetic response, and effective citizenship) and there is campus-wide assessment of achievement in those areas. It is not a question of developments in the teaching, learning and assessment arrangements in one area being of a different order to those in others, with some being untouched by any pedagogic thinking since the 1950s: *all* are engaged in practical, 'action' research into student learning and into teaching. Other American HE institutions have followed suit, with King's College, Pennsylvania emphasizing values awareness, information technology, critical thinking, writing, oral communication, creative thinking and problem-solving, computer literacy, and information technology.

The need for a systems approach

But why should assessment *systems* and *systemic* approaches to assessment be desirable, as this section is implying? We offer two educational reasons which focus primarily on student learning, following them with more managerial reasons.

Breadth and balance constitute one answer. If assessment is at the caprice of the individual tutor, there is little guarantee that students' learning, across their degree studies, will be broad in terms of the qualities which are developed, let alone balanced. What they learn to do will be arbitrary. Worse still, if tutors believe that the way they teach is the key variable in student learning and ignore the considerable impact that assessment arrangements have on the real curriculum, then there is every danger that they will unthinkingly take the line of least resistance on assessment and use the simplest or most traditional form. In other words, the curriculum will be narrowed because students will work to the narrowed assessment arrangements. A broad and balanced curriculum demands a broad and balanced assessment system.

Nor is it sufficient for any one department to ensure that its programmes reflect this happy state of affairs. Not only do CATs arrangements, unitization and modularization offer students considerable freedom to take courses in other departments, but the university surely also has a moral responsibility to ensure that no set of students is knowingly disadvantaged in comparison with any other group. In other words, there is an institutional duty to ensure that some minimum standard of breadth and balance is guaranteed. This is what the National Curriculum does for schools, although our argument is not that there should be such extensive prescription for HE. However, we do think that students should expect to develop a range of problem-working, communication and critical thinking faculties, and that it is not acceptable that only students in certain departments are assessed on those achievements, for that implies that only in those departments are those abilities taken seriously.

The second reason why a systemic approach is necessary is because, once it is accepted that a department is trying to develop certain understandings across three years, or that a university intends to foster general abilities in that time, the issue of *progression* arises. By progression we mean gearing the work – and the assessment – so that they demand that the student gets better (at some rate), rather than just havers for three or four years. Progression is about learning.

Clearly, progression implies an overview of the learning and assessment arrangements to ensure that students do not simply get one opportunity to work on oral presentations, working under just one set of constraints, displaying only one aspect of what they might learn to do. Progression is about building in opportunities for learners to show themselves to be virtuosos – or very much in need of more learning.

The very idea of progression self-evidently demands systems thinking, particularly as there are grounds for fearing that some manifestations of modularization may impede progression and fragment systems.

There are also pragmatic reasons for our stance. One is that student resistance to 'innovative' assessment processes will be minimized where these practices are part of institution-wide expectations and practices. A second is that there are efficiencies of scale to be had, not just in the economic sense that duplication of development, implementation and reaction can be minimized, but also in an academic sense. If students follow courses which reinforce similar points and which complement each other, then their learning may be efficient. Notice that we are not trying to imply that the content or perspectives of courses should converge, that students should all study medieval England before Hanoverian Britain, and that before the British Empire. Nor do we imply that they should not be exposed to competing sociological analyses in sociology, to differing paradigms in psychology, to various explanations of the nature of matter in physics. What we are saying is that there is an efficiency gain to be had if concepts fundamental to what it is to be a graduate are visited and revisited in courses in a systematic way, rather than haphazardly, coincidentally, or not at all.

Third, any decision to concentrate upon assessment, and by implication upon curriculum, teaching and learning, is an economic decision with its own opportunity cost. If we decide to spend time in that way, then it is not available for other activities, activities which the institution may value more highly. A department in an older British university may find it hard to reconcile the wish to have a strong research profile and to be innovative in teaching. The newest universities are continuing to try and win reputations for their research work. Different profiles attract different students, and a university which is distinguished for its assessment practices will find that it appeals more to some students and employers than do others. In each case the decision to spend time, and probably money too, on assessment is one which has implications for the system as a whole and which needs to be seen in the context of what that system is there to do. Regrettably, the only public source of guidance on that is mission statements.

Fourth, there is the accountability argument. A university, as a whole, is accountable for what happens within it. A system of assessment makes it possible to explain what students do and gain through their undergraduate experience. In the USA this has become very important, and Ewell and Jones

(1991a) have described how the development of assessment systems has been an important part of HE's demonstration that it gives value for money. The existence of a systemic assessment programme has also proved useful to individual institutions competing for state funding. The relationship with an institution's total quality management procedures will be addressed later.

Finally, there is a synergy to be had from creating an academic body in which most members take seriously the business of thinking about assessing and teaching students. Not only does this allow for ideas to be shared, for colleague to speak unto colleague, but it also has the potential to pull departments together in ways which academic research, by contrast, seldom does. A strength of HE is certainly the autonomy of the individual academic, but it is also its greatest weakness, as each re-invents the teaching wheel, pursues his or her own priorities, tries to teach students techniques which ought, surely, to have been learnt earlier, and fails to spark colleagues in that way which characterizes a community of learners. Checkland (1981), advancing his own notion of systems thinking, used the concept of 'emergent properties', roughly meaning the way in which a whole system can be more than the sum of its parts. In academic communities the possibility of emergence also exists – within departments, within universities and within networks such as subject associations and the EHE networks.

Difficulties with systems approaches to assessment

It might just be that the idea of assessment reform as a way of pulling scholars together while leaving them free in many areas of their work could be the most powerful and largely unexpected outcome of assessment reform. Desirable though it is for individuals to assess more imaginatively, it is better for departments to assess as departments and best for that to happen within a university-wide framework. We are conscious that the logic of this points towards a core, national HE curriculum of the sort which NVQs may become. That is not to say that we endorse that logic, and in Chapter 13 we shall discuss the matter further, putting it in the context of changes in HE generally.

Even in the USA, reports suggest that the ideal is often not achieved. Assessment takes place at a number of points within American HE, with much going on as a normal part of the teaching process within subject departments, while general testing programmes are also often administered by specialized assessment officers. Yet, so far from this being evidence of a systemic approach at work, Ory and Parker report that in large research universities 'one individual or office seldom knew about *all* assessment activities being conducted on campus' (1989, p.381). Underwood concurred, noting that in his university ' . . . rather than a university-sponsored alumni activity study, 20 alumni activity studies are being conducted by various departments and individuals across campus' (1991, p.65). While individuals may get useful data in this way, it is hardly efficient, nor is it easy to see how it will benefit the university as a whole.

Other weaknesses in the breadth and balance of assessments have been reported. There is some evidence that insufficient attention has yet been given to assessment *within* academic subjects (Sell, 1989), with much of the work on developing assessments of student learning outcomes being directed to assessing general transferable skills, competences and dispositions through discrete testing arrangements. A second principal focus is on using student evaluations to assess *teaching* quality, which is ironic, given that it is student *learning* which is at the heart of the enterprise. Indeed, Underwood (1991) found that although there is agreement that general education testing and value-added testing are of considerable importance, only five out of the 93 respondents in the New Mexico State University saw the former as an assessment priority, and one the latter. Seven saw assessment in the major subject as a priority. Underwood concluded that

while the non-cognitive areas seem to be well covered, some method must be devised to account for the cognitive assessment [but] . . . since cognitive outcomes are much more difficult, are more expensive and attempts to measure them meet with more resistance, the task is no minor undertaking (p.67).

A number of points of importance are raised by this. First, there is the matter of how to energize departments to take assessment seriously *and* to consider promoting and assessing cross-curricular, generic achievements. Second, there is the related issue of how to encourage a 'cross-connectivity', so that different programmes promote – and assess – the same core of general abilities, looking to document similar achievements in similar ways. Assessing such achievements is an issue of concern, for where a number of American universities do it through one standard, generic test, there is a case for saying that these general abilities are best assessed within a disciplinary context. The price of doing so is that it becomes impossible to compare students' performance on something such as critical thinking across departments, since the various tests will themselves have contributed to the variance in performances. Then there is the question of whether subject programmes ought to encourage a transfer of learning, that is to say, whether they should deliberately encourage students to apply principles and procedures from other courses and departments to *this* course, and *vice versa*. Finally, departments often lack the expertise to develop fair assessments of problem-working or oral communication.

So, what is meant by a system?

This reminds us that a major problem in the HE curriculum is the tension between the disciplinary interest in examining themes, problems and topics of interest, through which important general procedures and concepts may be learned, and the increasing demand that degree programmes be designed to promote systematically a range of procedures and concepts which may be widely applied, which the student is aware of having and is usually able to apply. The tension arises not because the two perspectives are incompatible, but because curriculum planning which starts from one perspective – be it the disciplinary or the procedural perspective – is likely to undervalue the other perspective. Given that most academics take their identity from their discipline, it is hardly surprising if it is the disciplinary perspective which predominates, leaving procedures to be identified through an academic 'hunt the thimble' afterwards.

There is a practical case, then, for saying that each academic unit (we have used the term 'department') might be regarded as a system. Were that so, we would be writing about departmental change and offering advice on departmental administration and micropolitics. And it is certainly true that when talking about changing systems we are talking about departmental change, and since academic departments continue to have noticeable freedom of manoeuvre, it is legitimate to see them as systems – to some extent. Since they form part of an institution with its own funding, leadership, mission (statement, at least), identity, procedures, bureaucracy and values, they may better be seen as sub-systems within what have been described as 'loosely-coupled organisations' (Orton and Weick, 1990).

The concept of loose-coupling means that there is considerable scope for initiative, priority-setting, action and identity, so that it is uncertain what the impact on any element of the organization of any particular action from the centre will be. This, incidentally, is not a deficit theory. Loose-coupling has many advantages as an organizational form, especially where people are the main organizational resource, where the business is non-routine (as professional work is) and where the predominant management assumptions are 'theory Y' (that people are self-motivated and capable, to be empowered rather than directed, supervised and controlled). Some consensus is necessary, and Peters and Waterman (1982) have said that successful organizations are characterized by simultaneous loose-tight coupling, where there is tight-coupling over goals and the ethos, co-existing with fluidity of approach. In other words, an effective system of HE will be diverse and tolerant of ambiguity in the pursuit of a commonly-held mission.

What we have, then, is a stance that assessment reform is a whole-university matter. Because universities tend to be loosely-coupled systems our systems thinking cannot be of the 'hard' mechanistic variety appropriate to solving well-defined problems in tightly-coupled systems, as with improving productivity in a factory. Rather, we need to use the problem-working methods of 'soft systems thinking' (Checkland, 1981). This means paying attention to the human dimension and accepting that 'solutions' are provisional and mutable. And this is why the university-wide focus is necessary, because at the heart of this view of change are meaning and values. This in turn provides another reason why a systems approach to assessment is necessary, for not only do we need an assessment system, but that system must feed – and be fed by – the other systems: we need a horizontal as well as a vertical integration, that is, to bring into a relationship all assessment systems, and to bring those systems into a relationship with teaching, research, counselling, careers development and relationships with outside stakeholders of all sorts.

Engaging academic staff in systemic changes in assessment practices

If universities are to become infused with the assessment ethic, a number of problems need to be faced (Ewell, 1988), especially:

- unclear motives: why is assessment being done? Without clarity – at least clarity about what the programme is *not* intended to do – it is hard to avoid conflicts and to mobilize support for assessment reform
- unknown consequences: including fears that the programme will be overblown or ruin the curriculum
- lack of authority: 'success will also require visible support from the institution's top leadership' (Ewell, 1988, p.18). In many American institutions this means that a vice-president has responsibility for assessment, and that there is an assessment officer and associated administrative support
- intimidation: existing programmes are complex and that makes it hard to begin a new programme and hard to know where to start, when and at what pace to move.

Other things might be added to Ewell's list, particularly the absence of assessment expertise among staff in general; the traditional lack of clarity about goals and aims; the tension between the individualist tradition among HE staff and the corporatist approach implicit in systemic assessment policies; reluctance to commit time and to take risks in an area which has had little importance in an academic career; academic resistance to external controls; and, by no means least, student resistance to new ways of doing things, to unfamiliar demands.

An oft-ignored difficulty is a product of cost-cutting. Writing of the USA, Gappa and Leslie (1993, p.232) said:

Of all the issues that arose during our site visits and interviews, perhaps the most alarming was the sense in some departments that their use of part-time faculty [tutors] had gotten out of control. Departments or institutions that felt that way exhibited some of the following characteristics: program decisions were made for fiscal reasons, planning horizons were short and externally driven, faculty staffing was ad hoc and driven by non-educational factors, policies on the use of part time staff were informal and capricious . . ., integration of part-time faculty into the institution and/or department was minimal, and evaluation of performance was erratic or non-existent.

Departments which employ many part-time staff are likely to find difficulty in achieving systemic change, certainly if part-time staff are not paid to take on the developmental responsibilities which attach to effective teaching.

There has been something of a tendency to see resistance to change as so many exhibitions of irrationality and self-interest, to be swept away by the use of rationality and power. The repeated failures of this technical-rational view of the change process have led to reappraisals of how change happens and of what happens to the change itself in the process of change. Fullan (1991) has emphasized that educational change is about changing people, particularly their values and beliefs, for without that, any changes in their behaviour will be shallow and perhaps deceptive. However, not only is it far from simple to change people, but it also implies that there are limits to what can be achieved by trying to impose one version of rationality (the university academic manager's) on another's (the mid-life lecturer's). To put it another way, there is limited mileage in trying to promote change by making a loosely-coupled organization significantly more tightly-coupled. In fact the attempt, impinging as it does on the existing culture, may well do more harm than good. Adopting 'theory Y' thinking, we see that in the process of trying to negotiate some shared meaning of what might be done, the change agent is likely to need to compromise, to accept that change will be slow, faltering and incremental, and settle for starting with changes in one area, preferably a non-threatening area (Year 1 assessment?) where success is likely.

Games academics play

Referring to assessment reform, Astin (1991) has illustrated this by referring to the games which academics play, ways of derailing someone else's plans. Rationalization (the proposal is unrealistic), passing the buck, caution, red herring and innuendo are some of the examples he gives of tactics which are used, wittingly or otherwise, to frustrate action. A powerful answer lies in selling to the department the idea that something needs to be done, that is, trying to build a shared commitment to the value of multiple assessment strategies. Of course, many departments know full well that something has to be done to manage student numbers, but they seem not to be so convinced that tinkering is not enough. But if they are to review their goals and assessment processes, there need to be offers of support, help on agreeing guidelines and constructive sympathy as they face a most complex task.

There is agreement that assessment programmes are most effective if academic staff are involved in their design, in their operation and in their review (Banta and Schneider, 1988; Sell, 1989). There are at least two reasons why. The first is that even if assessments do not deliver valuable data which are used, there appears to be an effect on teaching simply because thinking about assessment involves reflecting on teaching and learning, and so the whole thing can work rather like a giant Hawthorne effect (crudely the

Hawthorne effect says that most innovations look successful at first: it's the act of being innovative which seems to make the difference, not the exact innovation).

Second, it is held that to be valid, assessment programmes should be customized to the circumstances of an institution, faculty or department, for it is too easy to use standardized tests which yield reliable data of low validity and little significance for institutional development. Necessarily, then, academic staff are involved in assessment development.

Innovation and implementation

With the innovation planned, says Fullan, the change agent often eases up. Implementation, though, is a crucial stage. Not only does it need to be worked on every bit as hard as was the planning, but it is also a stage of further change. Implementation changes changes. Not surprisingly, many project evaluations which were looking for a 'goodness of fit' between the plan and the outcome found mismatches and concluded that the project had therefore failed in some manner, often blamed the implementers, who were typically teachers, and concluded that next time the solution would have to be a tighter-coupled system, by making the innovation 'teacher-proof', for example. The teacher-proofed projects also failed. Implementation is as fundamental to how the change turns out as is planning. The secret is to manage the implementation of an assessment plan as creatively as the original planning process.

Using these perspectives leads us to believe that a technical-rational approach to developing an assessment system, centrally-directed and imposed, is not appropriate to a system of professional activities. That is not to deny the importance of central initiative; of incentives; nor of the institution requiring that actions of a certain sort be taken. That would amount to a renunciation of the very idea of the university as a system with its own identity and culture. However, there is an important distinction between having a direction and being directed. A starting point might be to require that all departmental codes of practice set out what is done on assessment under certain headings, circulating copies to every other academic department, as well as to students.

Chapter 11:

Changing Systems

Ewell (1988) suggests a number of ways of making it more likely that reform will be fruitful:

- establish an assessment office or committee, carefully chosen and with powerful support from senior management
- prepare by doing a review of current practice
- run a pilot or demonstration project – start small
- make better use of information which is already collected
- rebut fallacies – for example the fallacy that there is 'perfect data'; that a single approach or indicator exists which will be sufficient; that high degrees of reliability and validity are *necessarily* needed
- as a matter of routine, use assessment data in planning and budgeting
- use assessment information in evaluations and programme reviews.

Again, we might add to Ewell's list; in particular, he writes from the perspective of the academic manager and places insufficient emphasis on making sure that teaching staff generally see that there are academic benefits to be had (and these may take the form of better student learning but, following Astin's dictum that 'good assessment is really good research' (1991, p.xii), they may also take the form of a new set of research possibilities for academic staff). Staff also should acquire some feeling of ownership of the development; they need to see that some resource support is available; that the programme can be amended as practical issues arise; that the data will not be used invalidly and to their detriment; and that teaching and curriculum development are more highly valued in the institution than the sop of the odd senior lectureship would imply. We note that there is a disincentive to reform in some institutions, where staff workload is calculated by contact hours, not by courses for which they are responsible. Consequently, the tutor who innovates and reduces the number of contact hours associated with one course is likely to be rewarded by being given an additional course to teach to make up the contracted workload.

Student resistance has been documented in the UK and the USA, but it has mainly occurred when a particular course was seen to be out of line with others, or when innovations were introduced to students already well-grooved into other routines and expectations. It is also likely to occur when new assessment arrangements are 'bolted on' to existing structures, so that students have to do more tasks. Where it is seen as a routine part of the business of learning, resistance is unlikely, although there may be criticisms that the precise tasks are faulty in some ways.

It makes sense to introduce change at the departmental level on an incremental basis, so that the new practices begin with a new intake in Year 1, start in Year 2 as they move into Part II and so on. Better still, involve the students in planning the new assessment system. Not only is this good politics, to give students some ownership, but it is pragmatic, since they will have invaluable points to contribute because of their perspective as the people who will be assessed in this way. That is also very consistent with current thinking about total quality management which sees the clients – students, in this case – as the people who are to be satisfied, and their satisfaction as the criterion by which we judge whether quality services are being provided. The belief that tutors and academic managers are there to serve the students implies that it is inconceivable that they would not be involved in such a major reform of the curriculum.

Change at the departmental level

Values may be centrally worked out, but they are extended and shaped in academic departments. We refer to them as 'holons', that is, as elements which can be regarded as systems in their own right, but which are also sub-systems. The increasing popularity of modular degree schemes which emphasize student choice has weakened the notion of the department with 'its' students: they are 'its' only insofar as they are taking at least one module under its aegis, a contrast with the older fashion for main subject departments in which a student took most of his or her courses and for whom the department was often given a pastoral as well as an academic responsibility. This means that when planning an assessment system, the department has to make certain assumptions about the modal route through its courses. This may involve a department in making rules that students who are taking at least half their courses within the department must take certain courses, not particularly because of the content of those courses, but because they have been designed to provide certain sorts of important assessment and learning opportunities. It will be appreciated that students who mix courses from several departments may well by-pass all plans for a coherence and progression in their assessment experiences.

Whatever, a starting point is to review aims and to consider assessment in relation to them in the systematic manner adopted by the geography department at S. Martin's College, Lancaster; this is shown in Table 11.1.

Assessment type	Assessment mode		
(M=monitoring)	*Self*	*Peer*	*Staff*
Examination			*
Essay	*		*
Seminar	*	*	M
Individual Project	*		*
Group Project	*	*	M
Oral Presentation	*	*	M
Report/Review	*		*
Practical/Field File	*		M
IT File	*		*
Field Course File	*		*
Portfolio			*
Dissertation Proposal			*
Dissertation			*
Placement Proposal			*
Placement Diary	*		M
Placement Report	*	*	*

Table 11.1 *The assessment system for geography, S. Martin's College, Lancaster*

As has been hinted, there is agreement in the literature that valuable and powerful effects of getting departments to do such an exercise, to address assessment seriously, include:

- making them consider their aims in some detail. Once aims are linked to assessment, some sharp thinking is needed, since invariably aims have to be refined, tightened and perhaps reconceived as academics wrestle with the issue of what would constitute a fair test of the aim and a suitable display of performance
- making them trace which of their goals is advanced in which parts of their programmes. This frequently exposes a highly uneven pattern of coverage, with some goals receiving massive attention, whereas others are distinguished by their rhetorical presence and practical absence
- forcing a collective consideration of teaching and learning methods, since assessment questions are teaching and learning questions
- sharpening understanding of the place and purpose of individual modules and units within the scheme of things, thereby making it possible to arrive at a more coherent view both of the programme and of the department (Astin, 1991; Banta and Schneider, 1988).

Figure 11.1 (overleaf) shows a simple grid which might be used in such a review. On one dimension we have discipline-specific and institutional goals,* while the other lists the modules taught within the department. In its first form this grid would show which goal was being promoted in which module. The temptation should be resisted to claim too much for any one module. It is better for the grid to express the one or two goals with which any one module really does grapple.

At this point gaps in coverage and duplication (or is this progression in another guise?) need to be addressed. A department may decide that no action need be taken on the grounds that the gaps are defensible, given the students, the subject, the staff or the resources available. Alternatively, action may be taken to revise the curriculum.

In its second form (Figure 11.2) the grid still comprises a list of modules, but the other axis lists the range of assessment methods which might be used. Here the intention is to reveal the extent to which a narrow range of methods predominates, thereby denying students the opportunity to demonstrate some of their achievements and effectively sending them the message that these are not matters of importance. Typically, in the humanities and social sciences, essay work will prevail, with there being few cases where self- or peer assessment, or project, simulation, oral and IT-based assessment tasks are used. Where a university has a commitment to promoting the wider range of abilities which are associated with this wider range of assessment techniques, then such a finding would be worrying.

Problems are by no means over, since there remains the question of standards. A benefit of a departmental approach to assessment is that it helps academics to become clearer about their colleagues' understanding of what matters. One facet of this is negotiating the meaning of the goals which have been set. If one goal is critical thinking, then what would be taken as sufficient evidence of critical thinking at this level? With a cross-curricular achievement such as this the answer will in part be worked out at university level. None the less, it also needs to be resolved at departmental level, for the goal takes on its full meaning within the disciplinary context. So, once the second grid is completed, gaps filled or accepted, a department will

---

* We learned of the MENO project after this book had been sent for typesetting. Its aim is to encourage the assessment and teaching of general thinking skills – namely, communication, literacy, numerical and spatial operations, understanding argument, critical thinking, problem-solving, and academic and professional effectiveness. These seven might be a useful starting point for a department considering the general abilities that might be specifically addressed in its programmes. While the MENO project has undoubted strengths, there are also problems, which we cannot discuss in a footnote. Further details from the University of Cambridge Local Examinations Syndicate, Cambridge, CB1 2EU, UK.

Outcomes	Discipline (1)	Discipline (2)	Discipline (3)	Discipline (4)	Problem Working	Creativity	Evaluation	Critical Thinking	Concise Expression	Information Handling
Course U201										
U203										
U204										
U206										
U301										
U303										
U305										
U310										
U311										

Figure 11.1 *Planning grid: courses and aims*

OUTCOMES ASSESSMENT METHOD	Discipline (1)	Discipline (2)	Discipline (3)	Discipline (4)	Problem Working	Creativity	Evaluation	Critical Thinking	Concise Expression	Information Handling
Project										
Constrained response										
Seminar presentation										
Timed essay										
Multiple choice										
Production of a reader										
Exhibition										
Poster										
Display of practical competence										
Case Study Analysis										
Portfolio										
(Laboratory) Logs & diaries										

Use **S** to show Self-assessment
Use **P** to show Peer assessment
Use **T** to show Tutor assessment

Use **E** for examination/exam equivalents
Use **U** for ungraded (qualificatory) assessment

Figure 11.2 *Planning grid: programme aims and assessment methods*

proceed to establish criteria of competence on the various assessments of the several goals. To repeat, this may be the most valuable outcome of thinking about assessment.

The department will have problems. In particular, there is likely to be a lack of assessment expertise, which leads to a lot of frustration and wasted time. It may also be that departments are not used to working on such complex issues and that they badly need facilitators who can help with group dynamics in a threatening situation where outcomes are expected, not paralysis. American experience is that departments then tend to construct assessments which emphasize the lower-level operations, neglecting the more advanced aspects of the discipline (Banta and Schneider, 1988). Eraut (1993, p.17) says that 'it must be recognised that designing an assessment system demands specialist expertise'. It is to that we turn, leaving to one side, for the moment, the matter of what departments might do with all the assessment data they will collect.

Assessment officers and administrative support

American universities tend to have a university assessment officer and an assessment office, although some English colleagues see that as a proliferation of bureaucracy and something else taking resources away from the sharp end of teaching. That ought not to be the case, since this senior management function appears to combine a lot which already comes under the headings of staff development (acting as change agent and facilitator), planning officer (analysing patterns of performance), examinations secretary and student records. In the previous section we argued that if departments were to develop their own assessment scenarios within an institutional ethos, then they would need support of exactly the sort which a central assessment office should provide.

Assessment officers, according to Astin (1991), need to have vision, an understanding of the academic world, a functional knowledge of measurement and of research design, technical know-how, understanding of the social science concepts relevant to measurement, teaching and learning, good communications skills and academic credibility. To that we would add skill in acting as a change agent, particularly skill in managing tense and threatening interpersonal situations. Assessment officers will also need to be fluent in explaining the rationale for assessment reform, since academic colleagues are accustomed to taking little on trust and will need to be persuaded that change is for the better. Once systems are up and running, administrative skill will be needed – as indeed it will be in the design of a university database – and the officer will have to be able sensitively to take analyses back to departments for their consideration and action.

This is a formidable job description. At present, different people in universities have different parts of the necessary expertise. Staff development officers have many of the skills, although some are not so familiar with such a pro-active role. Administrative officers will also be needed who will have to acquire expertise with the information-handling system. Two implications strike us. One is that this job has to be conceptualized as a teamwork. The second is that the work of staff development workers is going to have to be rethought in all sorts of ways. It will be professionally useful for them to become fluent in the intricacies of assessment.

We have taken a view of assessment which is wide-ranging, explaining that we see it providing information of considerable value for many purposes. A strong system of academic counselling is needed if the benefits of broad, criterion-referenced assessment are to be realized within a modular, unitized system in which students have many choices open to them. The academic counsellor will clearly need to have access to full and up-to-date information about the student's achievements in all areas. It is far from clear that existing counselling systems have kept pace with either the increase in student numbers or the proliferation of options available to students. A result may have been to empower the student, in the sense of giving him or her freer choice, but at the expense of empowering the student by ensuring that he or she has acquired certain abilities which are valued and valuable.

Such a counselling system may have powerful implications for the way student records are kept and handled. Much data on students are duplicated across the university and most of them are fragmented. Often it is only the student who has a fairly complete picture of his or her own achievements. Bearing in mind the provisions of the Data Protection Act, universities must investigate ways of bringing together information about students.

That also allows analyses to be done in the interests of improving institutional performance. Finding out whether coursework marks are much different from examination marks is, by itself, a laborious task at most universities. Looking at subsets of that data – analysing it by department, by age of student, by gender, by year of course – is Sisyphean. Yet, if an institution is to grow it needs such information, and could easily get it from a well-designed, well-maintained data-handling system. We shall shortly develop this point.

Which assessment data are useful?

Before looking at the uses of these data, it is important to think about the *form in which the data ought to be analysed*. It is well known that simply judging an individual, department or institution in terms of their (or their students') attainment is naïve, since this ignores the question of how good the students were to begin with. While A-level scores are not good predictors of degree class, they are as good as any other predictor and better than most. So, a student with good A levels is more likely to get a good degree than one with poor A levels. Consequently, if universities make judgements about departments without making allowance for the characteristics of the student intake, they are not only judging unfairly, but they are in danger of failing to recognize areas of excellence and areas of indolence: the department with good intake and modest student degree grades needs attention, but of a rather different sort to the department whose students have poor A levels but who do equally well in finals. 'Added value' is what we should analyse, and it was in that spirit that Peter Knight once had a policy of admitting students with the most modest A-level scores. Astin (1991) is insistent that universities should be judged neither by the quality of the student intake, nor by the quality of the degrees gained by its graduates, but rather by their success in talent development – that is to say, by the effects universities have had on students during their programmes of study. He noted that these effects bore 'a weak relationship, if any, to [an institution's] level of resources or reputation' (p. 7).

Unfortunately, while the concept is appealing, the practice is appalling. Let us leave aside the problem raised by non-standard entrants, overseas and mature students. Let us also forget that students may have anywhere from 6 to 30 A-level points, but that there are effectively only five degree classes, which makes correlation rather clumsy. More important is the question of how we calculate added value. One solution is to say that a first is worth, say, 50 points, a 2:1, 40 and so on. The problem with this is that it is arbitrary: who says that a first is worth 20 points more than three grades of A at A level? There will certainly be well-known statistical quirks at work, ensuring that high-scoring students have less chance of maintaining excellent grades than modest students have of improving theirs. Simple though this system may be, it is arbitrary and produces anomalies (PCFC, 1990). Even so, it is, in our view, preferable to depending upon raw score data.

An alternative method for calculating added value is preferred by the PCFC/CNAA team, but is not without its problems. Essentially, the performance of an individual, department or university is judged by seeing how it compares with what might have been expected, when taken in the context of the performance of all similar individuals, departments or universities in previous years. Was the performance better or worse than might statistically have been predicted? Plainly this is mathematically complicated and depends upon a national database. Furthermore, by definition it ensures that as many will fall below average as rise above it: losers are in-built.

We know of no entirely satisfactory way of responding to the common-sense proposition that departments should be judged according to the difference which they have made to students. Probably it is best to go for relatively crude, easy-to-apply formulae, as long as they are used in the knowledge that they are better than raw score data but still far from perfect.

Using assessment data

The American experience of wide-ranging, add-on programmes is that it is not always easy to get students to engage with the extra assessment activity (Erwin, 1991). Besides, assessment, as we have noted, is often traditional and narrow in form (Ory and Parker, 1989) and does not allow institutions to measure 'added value', nor to show student cognitive growth. It is hardly surprising, then, that universities are seldom good at using assessment data: 'an institution that effectively practices assessment for both improvement and accountability . . . is an ideal that few have realised' (Sell, 1989, p.28). We have already noted that, as it is, little use is made of information gained through assessing students. We have also set out a case for raising the importance of assessment on the grounds that it can provide information which is of considerable use to many parties and which is important for many reasons, not least because it can help to develop teaching and enhance the quality of student learning. The whole enterprise will founder, though, if there is no agreement about using the hard-quarried assessment data.

Assessment data have the potential to provide valid performance indicators about the core business of HE: teaching and learning. With the reservations already expressed, these data serve as grist for:

- departmental review
- quality audits and total quality management
- course validation and re-validation
- course design, especially where inter-disciplinary degrees are projected
- programme evaluation
- university development plans
- publicity and institutional promotion
- student academic, careers and 'pastoral' counselling; hence student recruitment.

Notice that we have excluded staff appraisal from this. The reason is that when we get to the level of the individual course and when something as important as a person's professional development is at stake, the unreliabilities in the system mean that it is wise to be careful. First, unless a tutor takes large groups, the chances of any pattern of results occurring by chance in any given year are quite high. Second, some courses may tend to attract certain types of student who are not representative of the population following a programme. A course on Louis XIV which demands a reading knowledge of French will attract a different group to one on popular culture in post-war England. An added-value approach may control for some of those differences, but crudities in that approach have been noted. A third reason for being careful takes us back to a fundamental assessment problem in the universities: how can we be sure that the same standards are being applied? It will be recalled that the A-level boards operate sophisticated procedures to try to bring different syllabi and subjects into line. Even there, unease persists. In the universities even double-marking of all assessed work appears still to be exceptional. Ensuring parity of standards is left to external examiners, who probably couldn't do the job well, as the system stands, and who do not, anyway, see that as their main function (Wisker, 1993).

Yet, all the time that assessment data are used in the knowledge that they are, at most, the best approximations of student performance that it is worth affording, then they are invaluable. Moreover, a university developing a programme on the lines of the points made in this book would be possessed of better information than its competitors, and be well placed, therefore, to make better decisions than competitors. Using this information depends, crucially, on designing-in ways of using it. If, for example, information about a student's achievements is collected but there is no way of reporting this usefully to employers and others, then, from that point of view, the data might just as well not exist. Equally, if departmental reviews fail to take account of the best information available about added value over the past five years, then they are severely limited in the conclusions which may be drawn. And again, decisions about resource investment will indeed be related to the level of demand for certain courses and to the strategic profile a university wishes to adopt, but it should also depend upon having a view of which departments do well at teaching and which need development, which will need investment of one sort or another.

The data will be used at several levels within the university. Assessment officers will summarize them, producing institutional profiles and identifying areas of interest, always bearing in mind that departments which recruit well-qualified entrants will find it hard to show a corresponding level of added value, when the outcome measure is degree class. Departments, enjoined to review their courses annually within the academic audit framework, will use assessment data in these reviews. Now, we agree that 'we often focus more on *getting* good ratings than on actually *learning* from them' (Astin, 1991, p. 183). Departmental reviews can easily focus on 'problems' and ignore the value of learning from successes, which we believe is a faulty approach. The view of assessment as research, of assessment data as information from which to learn, is fundamental to using assessment productively, whether at departmental or at university level. An outcome will probably be course revision, which is a part of normal, natural life in any case. Given that the philosophy of total quality management is that excellence is designed in, problems designed out, it follows that assessment data will be an important prompt for reflection in course design. It is probable that assessment officers might be invited to contribute to this process of review and redesign.

However, early indications from the ALTER project, directed by Drs Brown and Partington, indicate that examinations officers in British universities have a clerking sort of organizational job, and operate procedures and maintain records, but do not have a place in the development and design of assessment policy. Furthermore, university records are not computerized in a form which allows much useful analysis to be done, nor are they readily accessible to the people who would benefit from proper access. We suggest that universities ought to consider seriously the data they need to have on student performance, who needs access to them and for what purposes. At its simplest, a lot of duplication of effort would be saved if departments adopted a common software package for handling student marks and used a standard template when doing so. In this way marks could be transferred and stored electronically, with only one set of keystroking to be done. This might have the advantage of exposing anomalies in the different assessment rules applied in different departments, encouraging the development of an institutional view of the core requirements for the award of a Bachelor's degree.

Systems analysts should be employed to ensure that this valuable information is organized in ways which give universities powerful indicators of how well they are doing. It is worth remembering that in institutions committed to total quality management, 'a critical aspect . . . is . . . the systematic recording of what is happening and the use of these records to feed-back information about what is happening' (Murgatroyd and Morgan, 1993, p.76). This makes sense, because if assessment systems are to contribute considerably to university decision-making, it is important that the data they produce are seen to be fairly gathered and properly used. Prehistoric information-management systems can discredit modern assessment practices.

Chapter 12:

Constraints

Staff

One of the main barriers to innovation in assessment will be academic staff. Some will not see the need; some will be wary of the purposes and implications of change; while others will simply lack the technical knowledge to move from the rhetoric which they accept to the reality which needs to follow. 'Managing academics is like herding cats', it is said. There is, then, a substantial, hope-filled, staff development job to be done. Realistically, though, we need to keep in mind Fullan's injunction, 'do not expect all or even most people or groups to change' (1991, p.106). This does not mean that it is idle to look for institution-wide reform, but it does mean that it takes years for new ways to become entrenched, and even then there will be colleagues who conform outwardly only and not at all if they can. Remember that in education 'people have always exercised the right not to implement priorities selected by external authorities' (Fullan, 1991, p.348). To repeat a point: wherever promotion rests on research records alone, and if teaching is conceived of only as performance in front of students, forgetting the significance of curriculum design, then it is not surprising if tutors tend not to accept the priorities which university management claims to have identified.

This raises questions about what form this staff development might take, to which we can refer only briefly here. Given our line that there is a substantial job to be done at departmental level and that only tutors in departments have the expertise to do it, it follows that staff development could usefully take the form of supporting departments with expertise in assessment, through consultancy. There also needs to be awareness-raising work, which might take the form of seminars, presentations and written material. Evaluation activities would be worthwhile, too.

Economics

It also raises, again, the whole question of costs. American costings vary depending on which costs are charged to the assessment programme rather than being borne elsewhere, by departments, for example. Estimates differ, typically ranging from 4 to 8 per cent of a programme's costs (Lewis, 1988). Universities in the USA also subsume more things under their heading of 'assessment' than we do, and their assessments often involve using commercially produced tests of general skills. A British university could expect to develop a new assessment system much more cheaply than its American counterpart, mainly because the programme would be more modest. There will, nevertheless, be costs, notably opportunity costs and staff development costs. Moreover, some 'new' assessment methods can be expensive, as the experience of NVQs has shown.

Assessment processes are seen to be time-consuming, typically involving candidates' supervisors in lengthy observation of activity. And time, of course, is money. Organizations are frequently unclear about the benefits they are getting from such an investment. This reinforces our point that we need to look at whole systems and, at the very least, to balance increased assessment costs in one part of a programme with reduced costs elsewhere.

It will have become clear from this book that we believe that assessment reform is necessary, is within the grasp of all academics, but is quite complex. It requires time and thought, and has ramifications for teaching and learning practices which will occupy further time and thought. Some colleagues will be unsettled by it, while others will become enthusiastic and spend more energy on pedagogy and assessment than on their 'native' subject. While assessment reform should save time in the medium term, it is heavily 'front-loaded' and demands a lot of time and acumen in the early years. In Chapter 7, MCQs were mentioned as an example of the high cost of developing some assessment programmes.

All of this represents an opportunity cost. In some cases the cost may be hidden from the institution, since colleagues sacrifice leisure time in order to take on the new demands, while maintaining their earlier activities. This has happened in many schools with the introduction of the National Curriculum. There are limits to the viability of this strategy, particularly as research is almost a leisure activity for many lecturers. And it is research which is the most likely casualty if tutors are diverted to pedagogic concerns, which is an uncomfortable conclusion at a time when a number of new British universities need to establish their credentials as 'real' universities by getting good research ratings. Since research is also a source of psychological rewards to many academics (material rewards being in rather short supply nowadays), it is easy to see that assessment reform could have substantial costs.

This is reflected in universities' confusion about their role. Discussing assessment, Atkins et al. (1993) argued that HE had at least four purposes: the general knowledge experience; preparation for knowledge creation; specific vocational/professional preparation; and preparation for general employment. Different aims imply different assessment mixes, of course, but they also lead to different priorities among staff, which means that some will take teaching and assessment reform more seriously than others. The latter may see these reforms as positively anti-educational, viewing them as they will through the lens which filters out all bar one purpose of HE.

One way of alleviating these opportunity costs is by employing part-time staff to take on some of the tutors' teaching load. Since they are not regally paid, this is hardly a high-cost strategy, but it is not cheap either, and makes it quite clear that reform of the curriculum and assessment is not a free lunch for university managements. Against those costs should be set considera-tion of the benefits of assessment (Ewell, 1991; Lewis, 1988), which may mean trying to put some kind of value on things such as the associated student and staff learning, enhanced standing for the institution, improved accountability, efficiency and effectiveness. As noted above, it is not axiomatic that improved assessment programmes necessarily bring these benefits, let alone that all of these benefits are valued. What is clear is that 'when the costs of evaluation start to exceed its [informational] benefits, no further evaluation should be carried out' (Lewis, 1988, p.72). Where this point lies will depend very much on the *use* which an institution makes of the data which are collected, which in turn implies that data-handling and use need to be considered when assessment programmes are being designed. And we have seen that there is evidence (Astin, 1991) that it is not usual to design systems which make appropriate use of assessment data.

Assessment reform will necessarily entail curriculum reform, which will also have its costs. Almost inevitably it shifts attention from teaching to learning, encouraging student self-sufficiency as a main goal. Flexible learning and assessment reform go hand-in-hand, and with them go demands on information sources, notably libraries, computer networks and other data archives. Work-based assessment implies work-based learning, which may carry new costs, while practical assessments imply field trips, laboratory and other practical work, with attendant costs. Oral presenta-tions imply that there is visual material for students to present and adequate supplies of flipcharts, OHPs, photocopying facilities and the like. Assess-ment and curriculum reform may save staff time (freeing them to do more teaching? – hardly a good incentive for reform!) but the savings are at the price of spending more on resources. This should still produce a net saving, and is in any case defensible on educational grounds, but it will not be a large, obvious saving. Indeed, continuing increases in group sizes may serve to hide the savings entirely.

Assessment reform needs a budget.

Expectations

A further constraint on assessment is excessive expectations. Let us be clear that we see assessment development as the most powerful instrument for change in HE. Yet, assessment data do not *prescribe* any one course of action.

It provides imperfect data which are to be interpreted. Policy decisions are then negotiated around the interpretations.

The research selectivity exercise done in England in the late 1980s assessed some departments as strong in research and others as weak. Universities differed in their policies in response to these assessments, some deciding to put money into strong departments to maintain their reputation, others to fund weak departments to improve their standing. So too with improving student learning. There is no simple connection between provision and student learning, not least because different institutions have different views of what sort of learning – and what sort of student – they wish to foster. If the aim is to improve student performance in a given area, there is no one way of doing so. A powerful strategy, used by many EHE directors, has been to invite target departments to bid for supplementary funding with a view to producing improvements in certain areas of student performance. Using assessment data is an art, a political art, in that it involves making value-led decisions. It would be damaging to assessment reform if it were believed that better data will be a panacea for institutional development. We would hope that academics are too sophisticated to have this 'perfect data fallacy'. If they do, it is a constraint on the development of an assessment system since it will always be seen to fail in their eyes. It is therefore important that people are clear about what better data cannot do, as well as about the benefits.

Standards

Over the past decade there has been a notable increase in the proportion of 2:1 and first class degrees awarded (Knight, 1991; Tarsh, 1990). In 1992 an education minister, Mr Forman, expressed publicly a concern that standards were being devalued and that what looked like a great triumph for HE in fact represented a decline in rigour, a relaxation of standards. Universities, he said, needed to demonstrate that this was not true. Ewell and Jones (1991a; 1991b) noted that in the USA there were fears that HE institutions would deliberately seek to manipulate performance measures without actually making any difference to the underlying performance, and also that necessary academic hurdles would be dismantled in the interest of allowing more people to graduate.

The phenomenon is indisputable, the causes contentious. One explanation involves the assessment system. As assessment requirements have placed more weight upon coursework, so student achievement has appeared to improve. The assumption is that coursework is rather 'easier' than examinations, which may be true (although an analysis of some Lancaster results in 1991 found that coursework appeared to get just an extra couple of percentage points and that in few cases would examination-only assessment have led to lower degree classifications). Even if it is true, it still begs the reliability issue, namely, which is the better indicator of what a student knows, understands and can do. In addition, the graded assessment of oral and practical competence has been seen as inflationary, especially where oral performances are marked on a grid and where students regularly tot up marks of over 70, rising into the 90s, even, which is unheard of in humanities and social science marking. Finally, it is possible that assessment requirements have become more 'student-friendly'. In the North West, for example, Peter Knight has observed the continuing reduction of the coursework load on students, as measured by number of words and number of items required. Again, it is not evident that this necessarily works in students' favour, since it reduces their opportunities to gain strong marks, albeit while attenuating the phenomenon of regression to the mean.

We also note that the accreditation of prior experience and learning (APEL) means that the length of a student's degree course may be substantially cut and that they might get their degree on the basis of fewer graded assessments than their colleagues. Given the considerable enthusiasm that there is for APEL, growth can be expected.

The point is that assessment reform has been associated with the 'inflation of degree grades'. It may offer some colleagues inspiration as a way of improving their students' ostensible (and actual!) performance. It is unlikely to be unwelcome to any HE institution, in the current climate. However, it reveals one line which colleagues wishing to resist assessment and curriculum reform might take, that is, to argue that it represents an erosion of standards. There is also the possibility that this might be an issue which attracts political attention, in the same way as the improvement of GCSE grades is a matter of concern to right-wing commentators.

Perhaps it is incumbent on the opponents of multiple assessment strategies to show that these strategies are associated with a decline in standards; perhaps this is not really an issue at the moment. But it may just become one, and if NVQs at Level 5 do become current in HE we can expect a lively debate as to what constitutes fair ways of assessing competence. Since NVQs, or perhaps GNVQs, will be the closest we have to a national curriculum for HE, it is not inconceivable that there could be government involvement at that point.

More prosaically, external examiners need to be convinced about the fairness of assessment methods, rules and weightings which will often be unfamiliar to them. They are constrained by the procedures validated by the university but, since they exercise considerable discretion in adjudicating borderline cases, there may be problems where an examiner is fundamentally unhappy with the general procedures and, as a result, is inclined not to give students the benefit of the doubt. For this reason, if for no other, it makes good sense to involve externals at the validation stage and to ensure that they have plenty of opportunity to see the rigour and validity of any new assessment procedures. At Alverno College external assessors have to participate in a training and induction programme to orient them to the institution's goals and standards. Since these externals are often not full-time academics, this system may not be appropriate for British external examiners, but we believe that the system as it stands is not satisfactory, retaining the weaknesses of role ambiguity without any obvious benefits.

For many departments professional bodies can be a constraint. Little can be said here, although we have a strong suspicion that it is not unusual for departments which are reluctant to change to use their professional bodies as ramparts, where in fact these bodies are quite amenable to discussing the good sense of innovations in curriculum and assessment. Most professional bodies are concerned to know that new entrants will make good *practitioners*, which does involve making sure that they know enough to practice. It also involves, as these bodies generally recognize, ascertaining that they can *practise*, that is to say that they have the personal and problem-working abilities which are the quintessence of effective work in fuzzy situations, in which the problem may not be clear, let alone the solution. Patently, assessment systems need to be imaginative if they are to document such professional competence, with the implication that many professional bodies, so far from being bulwarks against innovation, have a vested interest in being convinced of the necessity of assessment development. Unfortunately, effective access to these bodies is often only through those colleagues who cite them as unyielding opponents of anything to do with the late twentieth century.

Modularization

We believe that a constraint on innovation reform which is potentially far more serious is modularization. We are not, to be sure, saying that modularization will necessarily hamstring attempts to put in place systems which embody diversity and progression, but we can see a great danger that they might. It may also lead to over-assessment.

Most British universities are either in the throes of modularizing or of unitizing their courses, or have already done so. There are many advantages to a system of modularized units, not least through advancing flexible access and transfer within and between universities. However, implementation of such a system throws up a multitude of problems in relation to assessment. We note concerns that:

- it will lead to 'log-jams' and bunching of assessments
- the range of assessment items will be restricted
- over-assessment will ensue
- the load on external examiners will become unreasonable
- students will deserve more academic counselling
- there will be validation problems.

Many courses have provided an assessment programme at the beginning of the term or year to avoid 'log-jamming' of assignments for staff and students. At best these have been imperfect systems, but they have at least made an effort to avoid peaks and troughs of workload. Under a modular system, students may be choosing courses across departments or indeed the whole university, and so it is unlikely that such planning of assignment timing will be feasible. It is easier to identify the problem than to resolve it. The logic of short modules is such that there is not much scope to ease the problem by the traditional device of telling students to plan their time better and to plan well ahead.

In some institutions, it is common to hear a call to use traditional examinations at the end of a semester as the main – or only – method of assessment. This is seen by some as the easiest way of coping in what they see as a fragmented system. We believe it is a trend to be resisted, because as we say elsewhere, the reliance on a single assessment methodology is highly disadvantageous to students. It also seems self-evident to us that not only would an examination-only system put a lot of extra strain on students, but also that the prospect of trying to turn round multiple sets of exam scripts in the limited time available at the ends of semesters would be a nightmare for lecturers.

Far better, we believe, is a system that combines a variety of methods including course-work and end-tests, so that workload is staged for staff and students. There are alleged difficulties about phasing course-work over a semester, because tutors may feel that it is impractical to assess too early and so there will be a tendency to cram the workload into the second half. It is possible, however, to put small, simple, early tasks together with pro-gressively difficult ones into a portfolio which is assessed *as a whole* at the end of a semester, but parts of which have been assessed at staged intervals.

Many fear that because individual units or modules have to be discretely assessed, this necessarily will mean that students will be assessed more. This does not have to be the case. Universities, such as Teesside, that have already modularized, set some assignments that integrate learning across modules and yet provide discrete elements of assessment linked to specific units. Where problems have been experienced, it has tended to be because course designers have been too ambitious in the scope of their planned assessments. We are sure that cherished traditions will have to be discarded: traditional three-hour exams are not appropriate for assessing every module, for example, and will often have to be replaced.

External examiners are valued agents of quality assurance under estab-lished systems but the cost of the current system has been called into question, and there have been problems too in finding and appointing external examiners in some subject areas. Put simply, examining is an onerous task undertaken for little remuneration, and increasingly aca-demics are assigning it a low personal priority.

Further problems are coming to light in universities where it is agreed that exam boards should be held at the end of each semester, thereby doubling the frequency of the duties. Other institutions have instead decided to continue to hold exam boards annually, but this in itself has inherent problems. For example, how will progression between units/modules be assured? If there is no mid-semester exam board, can students go on to the second semester with provisional success in units in the first semester? What about the student who has failed dismally in all or most units in the first semester? Should such a student be advised to leave at this point, or to struggle on, with no hope of completing the year successfully? As discretionary grants become more difficult to obtain for repeating students, the implications for students who complete and fail a full year are becoming increasingly severe. We feel that common sense must be used here.

In the past, students have been informally counselled early in the academic year if their achievement is dangerously poor. This, at the very least, must happen in a modular system but it can only be done if someone, somewhere, has overall responsibility for each student, and has a clear picture of overall achievement. Many modular programmes have not yet grasped the nettle of taking responsibility for individual performance under a fragmented system. At very least, we assert the need for mid-semester review of students' performances in each unit, with feedback given to students to help them to monitor their own performance.

Under a modular system it is assumed that each unit or module at the same level represents an equivalent level of achievement. However, units and modules are normally devised by individuals or teams who base their decisions on a combination of experience and pragmatism. Levels of achievement are commonly broadly in line with what was previously designated by year, Level One work being approximately at the level that first-years might achieve, and so on. However, a unitized or modular system usually provides opportunities for students to choose elective elements from across the university, and indeed between different universities. We believe that equivalence will necessarily be approximate, but the best assurances are provided by the use of learning outcomes and by effective cross- and inter-institutional quality assurance mechanisms.

Summary

The university which gets ahead and which lasts will, in most cases, have vigorously worked over its teaching practices. Assessment is fundamental to teaching. Get the assessment right and the teaching, by and large, follows. Trying to get the teaching 'right' without taking assessment seriously is an exercise in futility.

Contrary to the assumption implicit in many works on curriculum and assessment change, we have said that this is not a matter where it is sufficient to win the hearts and minds* of individual academics. System-wide change is necessary, and massive issues of priorities, purposes and practice loom. The university that lasts will now be wrestling with the pretty nasty problems which we have described and facing a period of reskilling, turbulence and, with luck, achievement.

---

* We have not relied on the formula that rational argument alone will win hearts and minds. The British government, with the National Curriculum, has done a lot to show that there is insight behind Lyndon B. Johnson's aphorism. As Gibbon said, we cloak it in the decent obscurity of a learned language. So, as translated by Terry Pratchett: 'Cuius testiculos habes, habeas cardia et cerebellum' (in Small Gods, 1992, p.341).

Chapter 13:

Conclusions

With what judgement ye judge, ye shall be judged: and with what measure ye mete, it shall be measured to you again (quoted by Shakespeare in *Measure for Measure*).

Haven't you heard how they work the tripos at Cambridge, my dear old boy? The night before the results come out, the old don totters back from hall and chucks the lot down his staircase. The ones that stick on the top flight are given firsts, most of them end up on the landing and are given seconds, thirds go to the lower flight and any reaching the ground floor are failed. The system has been working admirably for years (Richard Gordon, 1952, *Doctor in the House*).

Student assessment is at the heart of an integrated approach to student learning (Harvey, 1993, p.10).

Our theme has been that assessment – or measuring – sets the tone of the curriculum to such an extent that a university may be judged by the way it judges – or assesses – its students. Inept assessment systems betoken problems in a university.

A view of a future

An ageing population, high levels of unemployment and a public borrowing deficit all make it certain that pressure to reduce public spending will increase, and this will inevitably affect HE.

We can forecast that more people will stay in full-time education for longer, that we will all be looking for better education, that the cost of putting vital new technologies into education will be significant, that the burden of repairing sub-standard accommodation will remain high, and that the system will continue to be labour-intensive (and if special education gets to be taken seriously, it will become more so). In other words, the demands of the education system will remain high and a great deal more could reasonably be spent on education.

Whether education is able to secure more funds in the face of competition from other areas is a moot point. Whatever, it is unlikely that HE will see more funds from within the education budget. Consider the following figures supplied by Jeff Rooker, MP. A full-time nursery or primary school place costs the taxpayer about £1,400. For a secondary school the sum is £2,200; £2,700 for FE and £6–9,000 for HE, excluding Oxbridge. There is evidence that in terms of the general good, especially in terms of the behaviour of adolescents, investment in nursery education may be the best bet. In economic terms there is a case for saying that the UK is held back by the lack of technicians, that is, of people who would normally be educated in FE. We might also recall that the schemes whereby universities franchise their courses to FE colleges are attractive to these colleges because they can teach these courses so very cheaply. Over this decade we shall undoubtedly see a growth in FE-based degree-level work. Mr Rooker concluded that by the end of the decade FE and HE would have moved so close together 'that you'll not be able to see the difference' (1993).

The conclusion thus far is that there is unlikely to be more money for the current university system and there may well be less, in real or in relative terms, especially at a time of reduced national resources, as North Sea oil revenues decrease and the number of those employed in manufacturing declines.

We have argued that universities are going to be hard-pressed to maintain, let alone increase, their share of a pressured education budget. When you consider that university education, largely the province of the middle classes and still heavily subsidized by the taxpayer, can be portrayed as 'pro-rich', then the situation looks trickier, particularly as FE can be characterized as more 'popular'. Let us now consider two paths universities might take. One is to cut costs. The other is to attract non-governmental money into the system, perhaps through state-supported cost-recovery schemes. We have not forgotten assessment. Our argument is that both routes depend crucially on effective assessment systems of the sorts which we have described in this book.

Cheaper HE

Academics are increasingly being pressurized to teach more cost-effectively by, for example, teaching beyond the traditional academic year and making greater use of open learning materials. But it is impossible to redesign the curriculum without clear and appropriate assessment strategies.

Unless assessment factors are taken into account at the design stage, curriculum innovation, which is fickle enough anyway, will be fatally compromised, since there is a good chance that the curriculum will be proclaiming one set of messages and the assessment procedures will be compelling attention to a different set.

Opinion is being 'softened up' in preparation for the introduction of cost-recovery systems, in the form, for example, of a graduate tax, to ensure that students pay something towards their own higher education. Once the students become paying customers, universities will need to be much clearer about what they are *for*. If universities are required to justify their existence and to demonstrate what added value students gain from their programmes, then it must be the case that assessment procedures need to be able to document the match between claim and reality.

We recognize that there is the potential for conflict between academic freedom and the departmental and university imperatives. As some universities come to look more and more like residential sixth-form colleges, it is not clear that the concept of academic freedom has been sufficiently thought through. What, exactly, is academic freedom? Is it a right to enquire or a right to teach? If the latter, then problems loom, since it is quite likely that some universities, at least, will begin to take views as to what constitutes worthwhile education for undergraduates.

Implicit in this is perhaps the idea that some departments will be essentially teaching departments, although tutors cannot be prevented from doing research at the margins if their discipline is one which makes it possible to do unfunded research. This has interesting implications for the selection and professional development of such tutors and also for university funding, since teaching departments, presumably, are cheaper than research departments.

The government has shown signs of concern about the value of first degrees in several ways. One is the EHE programme, the largest and most systematic attempt to transform HE without legislation. Another is the development of NVQs. Conceptually, the two initiatives are intertwined. Our point about NVQs, which are an attempt to define certain competences which people of graduate standing might well have, is that they too are dependent upon assessment reform – predicated upon it. We are unsure whether NVQs, or more probably GNVQs, will become a national HE curriculum, and equally unsure about the merits of such a curriculum. However, we can appreciate that a university, wishing to establish its distinctiveness, could see considerable advantages to incorporating GNVQs and NVQs into the curriculum, allowing its graduates to compete in a difficult jobs market with the backing of nationally recognized statements of general (and desirable) competences.

Resources and staffing

We recognize a contradiction between foreseeing resource pressure and the proposition that we need to invest in assessment reform. We can only say that it is better to do it now than to tarry until the resource situation is too desperate for action to be possible. The main areas of concern are resource centres, especially libraries, and staff development.

Implicit in much that we have said is the idea that more diverse assessment arrangements will go hand-in-glove with flexible learning methods. At Lancaster, for example, pilot work is in hand which uses assessment reform as a way of allowing students to plot their own paths through the courses on offer, so that Part II courses might be taken in Year 1 and master's credits and publications might take up part of Year 3. If this is to work, if universities are to become learning resources rather than teaching places, then universities need to invest in micro-technology and books.

However, flexible learning programmes and innovative but more conventional courses take deep thought, consultation and expertise. There is no question but that innovation is hard, even for those who have a background in educational and professional development. Others may not even know what it is that they don't know – but need to. For this reason an urgent demand is for better and more extensive ways of staff and educational development. Present systems seem to fall somewhere between two unusable models: the course-led programme of instruction by experts, on the one hand, and the 'discovering the wheel' model on the other. The problem with this latter model is not so much conceptual as actual. In the event, what is often discovered is not the wheel but the octagon. We suggest that staff development might best proceed through supporting course development, but with the requirement that development teams have expertise in assessment to hand and that an evaluator is appointed to each team. A further requirement that relevant disciplinary bodies be consulted could also be useful.

If assessment is to be systemic, then institutions need to have coherent programmes to involve and reward part-time and full-time staff.

Academic professions

It might be objected that this is too costly and risks compromising universities' research ratings. In reply we could say that research does not bring the bulk of funds into universities, but we do recognize the importance for other reasons of doing well in research selectivity exercises. We also know how much the teaching burdens on tutors have increased of late. These changes parallel what has happened with school-teaching, what has been described as *intensification*. It is instructive to pursue the comparison, since teachers have lost some, arguably much, autonomy over the past decade and have been 'deprofessionalized', it is said. Teachers have lost control of curriculum planning (but not of delivery, nor of pedagogy) and of assessment. Their work has been increasingly regulated and they are located more firmly than before within bureaucratic control. It is plausible to attribute this to teachers' failure to reform their own practices in response to increasing concern about the practice of education. The early 1980s were years in which national curriculum developments were out of favour and school-based curriculum development (SBCD) was fashionable. Yet SBCD failed to deliver, providing uneven and marginal developments, which showed little sign of outside influence (Knight 1985). In the face of such inertia or misaligned energy, the government took it upon itself to define the goals and conditions of schooling.

The similarities with the situation in which HE finds itself are notable. We have seen that GNVQs offer the possibility of a core national HE curriculum. We suggest that if HE does not act imaginatively to do what the schools of the 1980s generally failed to do, then it faces a similar fate. The best defence against a hostile take-over is strong performance which pleases the shareholders. HE needs to take the initiative in ways which please the stakeholders; if they please academics too, so much the better.

Summary

We have looked into the future and argued that in ever more competitive times universities – both in concert and individually – will have to sharpen up their act if resources are to be preserved. Whether they respond by trying to be more efficient or by reforming the curriculum to make it clearer why HE is a good investment (for the individual and for society), or by both, we have argued that assessment reform is not only desirable but also necessary – although not sufficient in itself.

There are other reasons why we believe that. For example, accountability depends upon a flow of information. Shoddy accountability systems may be based on shoddy data, which means that assessment systems are also shoddy – and most likely the fault will be a validity fault. To rephrase it, quality assurance and control systems are only as good as the information upon which they are based. It seems rather odd that academics are so worried about assessments of teaching quality because they may be based on invalid and unreliable data, but that they are more muted when it comes to asking how valid and reliable their assessments of student achievements are.

But the most important reason for assessment reform subsumes this point. Assessment is at the heart of learning. Assessment is for learning. Assessment is learning.

References

Adelman, C (ed) (1989) *Signs and Traces: model indicators of college student learning in the disciplines*, Washington DC: Office of Education Research and Improvement.

Adelman, C (1990) *A College Course Map: taxonomy and transcript data*, Washington: US Government Printing Office.

Anastasi, A (1988) *Psychological Testing*, 6th edn, New York: Macmillan.

Andresen, L, Nightingale, P, Boud, D and Magin, D (1993) *Strategies for Assessing Students*, Birmingham: SCED.

Angelo, TA and Cross, KP (1993) *Classroom Assessment Techniques: a handbook for college teachers*, San Francisco, CA: Jossey Bass.

Arksey, H (1992) *How to Get a First Class Degree*, Lancaster: Unit for Innovation in Higher Education.

Arter, J (1990) *Curriculum-referenced Test Development Workshop Series, Addendum to Workshops Two and Three: using portfolios in instruction and assessment*, Portland OR: Northwest Regional Educational Laboratory.

Assiter, A and Shaw, E (1993) *Using Records of Achievement in Higher Education*, London: Kogan Page.

Astin, AW (1991) *Assessment for Excellence: the philosophy and practice of assessment and evaluation in Higher Education*, New York: Macmillan.

Atkins, MJ, Beattie, J and Dockrell, WB (1993) *Assessment Issues in Higher Education*, Sheffield: Employment Department.

Badley, G (1993) *Improving the Quality of Teaching and Learning in Higher Education*, Birmingham: Standing Conference on Educational Development.

Baldwin, C (1993) *A Comedy of Errors*, Lancaster: Lancaster University Students' Union.

Banta, TW (ed) (1988) *Implementing Outcomes Assessment: promise and perils*, San Francisco, CA: Jossey Bass.

Banta, T (1991) 'Linking outcomes assessment and the freshman experience', *Journal of the Freshman Year Experience*, **3**, 1, 93–108.

Banta, TW and Schneider, JA (1988) 'Using faculty-developed exit examinations to evaluate academic programs', *Journal of Higher Education*, **59**, 1, 69–83.

Becker, H (1968) *Making the Grade: the academic side of college life*, Wiley: New York.

Bodner, GM (1989) 'Model indicators of undergraduate learning in chemistry', in Adelman, *op cit*.

Boud, D (1990) 'Assessment and the promotion of academic values', *Studies in Higher Education*, **15**, 1, 101–11.

Boud, D (1992) 'The use of self-assessment schedules in negotiated learning', *Studies in Higher Education*, **17**, 2, 185–200.

Boud, D and Falchikov, N (1989) 'Quantitative studies of self-assessment in higher education', *Higher Education*, **18**, 5, 529–49.

Boud, D and Feletti, G (eds) (1991) *The Challenge of Problem-based Learning*, London: Kogan Page.

Boyd, H and Cowan, J (1986) 'A case for self assessment', *Assessment and Evaluation in Higher Education*, **10**, 3, 225–35.

Brown, G and Pendlebury, M (1992) *Assessing Active Learning, vol 1*, Sheffield: CVCP.

Brown, S and Baume, D (1992a) *Learning Contracts: A theoretical approach*, Birmingham: Standing Conference on Educational Development.

Brown, S and Baume, D (1992b) *Learning Contracts: practical examples*, Birmingham: Standing Conference on Educational Development.

Brown, S and Dove, P (1992) *Self and Peer Assessment: a guide for enterprising students*, Newcastle: University of Northumbria at Newcastle.

Brown, S and Maher, P (1992) *Using Portfolios for Assessment: a guide for enterprising students*, Newcastle: University of Northumbria at Newcastle.

Chambers, E (1992) 'Work load and the quality of student learning', *Studies in Higher Education*, **17**, 2, 141–53.

Checkland, P (1981) *Systems Thinking, Systems Practice*, Chichester: Wiley.

Cross, KP (1990) 'Assessment 1990: understanding the implications', Washington, DC: paper presented to AAHE conference on assessment.

Cross, KP and Angelo, TA (1988) *Classroom Assessment Techniques – a handbook for faculty*, Ann Arbor MA: National Center for Research to Improve Postsecondary Teaching and Learning.

Eisner, E (1985) *The Educational Imagination*, 2nd edn, New York: Macmillan.

Employment Department (1992) *REAL Paper 17a – identifying examples of good quality assessment*, Sheffield: The Employment Department.

Engineering Professors Conference (1992) *Assessment Methods in Engineering Degree Courses*, Bristol: EPC.

Entwistle, N (1993) *Recent Research on Student Learning and the Learning Environment*, Birmingham: paper presented to the conference of the Standing Conference on Educational Development.

Eraut, M (1993) 'Implications for standards assessment', *Competence and Assessment*, **21**, 14–17.

Eraut, M and Cole, G (1993) 'Assessment of competences in higher level occupations', *Competence and Assessment*, **21**, 10–14.

Erwin, TD (1991) *Assessing Student Learning and Development*, San Francisco, CA: Jossey Bass.

Esp, D (1993) *Competences for School Managers*, London: Kogan Page.

Evans, C (1993) 'The reflective practitioner, the institution and help from outside', in Knight, PT (ed) *The Audit and Assessment of Teaching Quality*, Birmingham: SRHE/Standing Conference on Educational Development.

Ewell, PT (1988) 'Implementing assessment: some organizational issues', in Banta *op cit*.

Ewell, PT (1991) *Benefits and Costs of Assessment in Higher Education: a framework for choice making*, Boulder CO: National Center for Higher Education Management.

Ewell, PT and Jones, DP (1991a) *Action Matters: the case for indirect measures in assessing Higher Education's progress in the national education goals*, Boulder, CO: National Center for Higher Education.

Ewell, PT and Jones, DP (1991b) *Assessing and Reporting Student Progress: a response to the 'new accountability'*, Denver, CO: State Higher Education Executive Officers.

Falchikov, N and Boud, D (1989) 'Student self-assessment in higher education: a meta-analysis', *Review of Educational Research*, **59**, 4, 395–430.

Forbes, DA and Spence, J (1992) 'An experiment in assessment for a large group', *CAP-ability*, 2 , 15–19.

Fenwick, A and Nixon, N (1992) *Profiling Work-based Learning in Academic Courses*, London: CNAA.

Fenwick, A, Assiter, A and Nixon, N (1992) *Profiling in Higher Education*, London: CNAA.

Fullan, M (1991) *The New Meaning of Educational Change*, London: Cassell.

Fulton, O and Machell, J (1992) *Enterprise in Higher Education: final report of the evaluation 1991–2*, Lancaster: EHE Unit, Lancaster University.

Gappa, J M and Leslie, D W (1993) *The Invisible Faculty: improving the status of part-timers in Higher Education*, San Francisco, CA: Jossey Bass.

Gealy, N (1993) 'Development of NVQs and SVQs at higher levels', *Competence and Assessment*, **21**, 4–10.

Gentle, CR (1992) 'Development of an Expert System for the Assessment of Undergraduate Projects – a case study', Nottingham: paper presented at Nottingham Polytechnic.

Gibbs, G (1991) 'Eight myths about assessment', *The New Academic*, **1**, 1, 1–4.

Gibbs, G, Jenkins, A and Wisker, G (1992) *Assessing More Students*, Oxford: PCFC/Rewley Press.

Goldfinch, J and Raeside, R (1990) 'Development of a peer assessment technique for obtaining individual marks on a group project', *Assessment and Evaluation in Higher Education*, **15**, 3, 210–31.

Grandy, J (1989) 'Models of developing computer-based indicators of college student learning in computer science', in Adelman, *op cit*.

Guildford Education Services Ltd (1993) *Directory of Computer Assisted Assessment Products and Producers*, Sheffield: Employment Department.

Harvey, L (1993) 'An Integrated Approach to Student Assessment', Warwick: paper presented to Measure for Measure, Act II conference.

Harvey, L, Burrows, A and Green, D (1992) *Criteria of Quality: summary*, Birmingham: QHE.

HMI (1991) *Aspects of Education in the USA: quality and its assurance in higher education*, London: HMSO.

Heywood, J (1989) *Assessment in Higher Education*, 2nd edn, Chichester: John Wiley and Sons.

Hounsell, D (1984) 'Students' Conceptions of Essay Writing', Lancaster: unpublished PhD thesis.

Hughes, I and Large, B (1993) 'Assessment of students' oral communication skills by staff and peer groups', *The New Academic*, 2, 3, 10–12.

Jenkins, A and Pepper, D (1988) *Developing Group-work and Communication Skills – a manual for teachers in higher education*, Birmingham: Standing Conference on Educational Development.

Jessup, G (1991) *Outcomes: NVQs and the Emerging Model of Education and Training*, London: Falmer Press.

Johnson, C and Blinkhorn, S (1992) 'Validating NVQ assessment', *Competence and Assessment*, 20, 10–14.

Johnson, R *et al.* (1991) *Assessing Assessment: an in-depth status report on the higher education assessment movement in 1990*, Washington DC: American Council on Education.

Jordan, TE (1989) *Measurement and Evaluation in Higher Education*, London: Falmer Press.

King, W, Gray, PF and Hossack, JDW (1992) 'Peer marking of technical reports', *CAP-ability*, 2, 20–25.

Knight, PT (1985) 'The practice of school-based curriculum development', *Journal of Curriculum Studies*, 17, 1, 37–48.

Knight, PT (1991) ' "Value added" and history in public sector higher education', *Public Sector History Newsletter*, 3, 1, 23–31.

Knight, PT (1993) *The Audit and Assessment of Teaching Quality*, Birmingham: SRHE/Standing Conference on Educational Development.

Lenning, OT (1988) 'Use of noncognitive measures in assessment', in Banta, *op cit*.

Lewis, DR (1988) 'Costs and benefits of assessment: a paradigm', in Banta, *op cit*.

McKeachie, WJ *et al.* (1986) *Teaching and Learning in the College Classroom: a review of the research literature*, Ann Arbor MA: School of Education.

McRae, J (1993) 'Self assessment and essential learning', London: paper presented to Higher Education for Capability Conference.

Machell, J and Fulton, KAO (1992) *Using Records of Achievement in Admissions to Lancaster*, Lancaster: Enterprise in Higher Education Unit.

Mahalski, PA (1992) 'Essay-writing: do study manuals give relevant advice?', *Higher Education*, 24, 1, 113–32.

Mallier, T *et al.* (1990) 'Assessment methods and economics degrees', *Assessment and Evaluation in Higher Education*, **15**, 1, 22–44.

Mazelan, PM, Green, DM, Brannigan, CR and Tormey, PF (1993) 'Student satisfaction and perceptions of quality', in Shaw, M and Roper, E (eds) *Quality in Education and Training*, London: Kogan Page.

Mitchell, L (1993) *NVQs/SVQs at Higher Levels: a discussion paper*, Sheffield: Employment Department.

Murgatroyd, S and Morgan, C (1993) *Total Quality Management and the School*, Buckingham: Open University Press.

Newble, D, Jolly, B and Wakeford, R (1993) *The Certification and Re-certification of Doctors: issues in the assessment of clinical competence*, Cambridge: Cambridge University Press.

Norman, GR (1991) 'What should be assessed?', in Boud and Feletti, *op cit.*

Oakland, J (1989) *Total Quality Management*, Oxford: Butterworth-Heinemann.

Orton, JD and Weick, D (1990) 'Loosely coupled systems: a reconceptualisation', *Academy of Management Review*, **15**, 2, 203–20.

Ory, JC and Parker, SA (1989) 'Assessment activities at large, research universities', *Research in Higher Education*, **30**, 4, 375–85.

Otter, S (1992) *Learning Outcomes in Higher Education*, London: UDACE.

Peters, T (1989) *Thriving on Chaos: handbook for a management revolution*, London: Pan.

Peters, T and Waterman, RH (1982) *In Search of Excellence*, New York, Harper & Row.

Polytechnics and Colleges Funding Council (1990) *The Measurement of Value Added in Higher Education*, London: PCFC/CNAA.

Pring, R (1991) 'Competence', Oxford: paper presented to the UCET conference.

Race, P (1992) *Quality of Assessment*, Pontypridd: The Polytechnic of Wales.

Race, P and Brown, S (1993) *500 Tips for Teachers*, London: Kogan Page.

Ramsden, P (1992) 'Lost in the crowd?', *Times Higher Education Supplement*, July 17, p.16.

Ridgway, J (1992) 'The Assessment of Teaching Quality', Lancaster: unpublished paper for the Faculty of Social Science.

Rooker, J (1993) 'The Future of HE and Training', Lancaster: presentation to The Future of HE and Training seminar.

Sadler, DR (1989) 'Formative assessment and the design of instructional systems', *Instructional Science*, **18**, 2, 119–44.

Sell, GR (1989) 'An organizational perspective for the effective practice of assessment', *New Directions in Higher Education*, **67**, 21–41.

Squires, G (1990) *First Degree: the undergraduate experience*, Buckingham: SRHE/Open University Press.

Stephenson, J and Laycock, M (1993) *Using Learning Contracts in Higher Education*, London: Kogan Page.

Stephenson, J and Weil, S (1992) *Quality in Learning: a capability approach to Higher Education*, London: Kogan Page.

Sternberg, R (1993) speech to CIBA foundation conference, London, 27 January.

Swanson, DB, Case, SM and van der Vleuten, CPM (1991) 'Strategies for student assessment', in Boud and Feletti, *op cit.*

Tarsh, J (1990) 'Graduate employment and degree class', *Employment Gazette*, 489–500.

Terwilliger, JS *et al.* (1989) 'A study of indicators of college student learning in physics', in Adelman, *op cit.*

Turner, K (1993) 'An Investigation of how Students Respond to Feedback on Coursework', Warwick: paper presented to the Measure for Measure Act II conference.

Underwood, DG (1991) 'Taking inventory: identifying assessment activities', *Research in Higher Education,* 32, 1, 59–69.

Verran, J *et al.*, (1993) 'Group projects in biological science', *The New Academic*, 2, 2, 9–11.

Whitaker, P (1993) *Managing Change in Schools,* Buckingham: Open University Press.

Williams, G (1993) *Identifying and Developing a Quality Ethos for Teaching in Higher Education*, London: Institute of Education.

Winter, R (1992) 'The assessment programme – competence-based education at professional/honours degree level', *Competence and Assessment*, 20, 14–18.

Winter, R (nd) *Outlines of a General Theory of Professional Competence,* Chelmsford: Anglia Polytechnic.

Wisker, G. (1993) 'Now you see it, now you don't: external examiners and teaching quality', in Knight, PT (ed) (1993) *The Audit and Assessment of Teaching Quality*, Birmingham: SRHE/Standing Conference on Educational Development.

Index